THE ACTS OF THE APOSTLES

Printed in Great Britain at the University Press, Cambridge
(Brooke Crutchley, University Printer)
and published by the Cambridge University Press
(Cambridge, and Bentley House, London)
Agents for U.S.A., Canada and India: Macmillan

THE ACTS OF THE APOSTLES

by

WILFRED L. KNOX, D.D.

Fellow of Pembroke College, Cambridge, Honorary Canon of Ely,
Formerly Scholar of Trinity College, Oxford

CAMBRIDGE

AT THE UNIVERSITY PRESS

1948

TO TONY

in return for many questions

CONTENTS

v

PREFACE

The substance of this book was delivered as a course of lectures at the Vacation School of Biblical Study at Oxford in August 1946. I must here express my gratitude to the members of the School for the patience with which they endured the lectures and for the improvements which I have been compelled to introduce in order to meet their questions.

I must also express my deepest thanks to the Principal and Librarians of the Pusey House for their kindness in allowing me to reside at the House during the period of the School, and for their unfailing readiness to allow me to waste their time.

WILFRED L. KNOX

Pembroke College
Cambridge

ABBREVIATIONS

C.A.H.   *Cambridge Ancient History.*

F.G.H.   *Fragmente der griechischen Historiker* (Jacoby).

H.T.R.   *Harvard Theological Review.*

L.S.J.   Liddell and Scott's *Greek-English Lexicon*, revised by Stewart-Jones.

T.W.z.N.T.   *Theologisches Wörterbuch zum neuen Testament.*

My books *St Paul and the Church of Jerusalem* and *St Paul and the Church of the Gentiles* are referred to as *Jerusalem* and *Gentiles.*

CHAPTER I

THE AUTHOR OF ACTS

The book of Acts professes in its opening sentence to be a continuation of the book which we know as the Gospel according to St Luke. We must not suppose from the fact that the preface in referring to the former treatise describing what Jesus 'began' to do and teach implies that the second treatise is intended to describe His later activity in the Church through the agency of the Holy Spirit. The word 'began' here, as often in the Gospels, is little more than an auxiliary verb (cf. Luke iv. 21, ix. 12).[1]

The risen Lord, exalted to the right hand of God, had received as a reward for His obedience the privilege of sending down to earth the Holy Spirit, Who was to carry forward on earth the work that He had begun; but the two stages were entirely distinct. The author merely intends to identify himself with the author of the previous treatise to Theophilus. The tradition that the author of the two treatises was Luke the beloved physician and friend of St Paul goes back to Irenaeus,[2] while we have evidence that the Acts was known and read in the Church as early as the writing of the letter of Polycarp (i. 2), who incorporates the words of Acts ii. 24 'whom God raised up, having loosed the pangs of Hades' (changing ἀνέστησεν to ἤγειρεν but otherwise quoting *verbatim*); it has made its contribution to the extraordinary medley of New Testament phrases and heathen religious and astrological language which

---

[1] Cf. Blass, *Grammar of N.T. Greek*, p. 227, n. 1, and Moulton and Milligan, *Vocabulary of the Gk. Testament, s. voc.*
[2] *Adv. Haer.* III, 1, 2.

NOTE

forms the Greek of Ignatius.[1] The book, if not 'Holy Scripture', was a Christian classic well before A.D. 117. In itself it professes, in virtue of its sudden introduction of passages written in the first person plural, to be the work of a companion of some of St Paul's missionary journeys, for this method of inserting passages written in the first person into a history generally written in the third is common in ancient historians.[2]

We have thus evidence as good as can be expected both for the antiquity of the book and for the belief that the author was a companion of St Paul, who also wrote the Gospel according to St Luke. As has been pointed out, there seems no reason why Luke should have been selected out of the Pauline circle except on the basis of a good tradition; if the author were unknown, we should expect the second century to have identified the author with a more prominent figure.[3] It is generally accepted at the present day. It has however been challenged fairly recently by the late Professor A. C. Clark,

[1] Since Ignatius rarely quotes, it is difficult to be certain of his sources. But for Ign. *ad Eph.* i. 2, δεδεμένον ὑπὲρ τοῦ κοινοῦ ὀνόματος καὶ ἐλπίδος, cf. Acts xxvi. 7 (vii. 2, Christ as παθητός, suggests Acts xxvi. 23, but is drawn from a credal formula); *ad Magn.* i. 2, καταξιωθεὶς γὰρ ὀνόματος, suggests Acts v. 41; v. 1, εἰς τὸν ἴδιον τόπον, is pretty certainly from Acts i. 25, as *ad Philad.* viii. 2, ἡ πίστις ἡ δι' αὐτοῦ is from Acts iii. 16; x. 1, ἐπὶ τὸ αὐτό = Acts ii. 47. Cf. also ἐκτενεία (*Magn.* xiv. 1) and μεμαρτυρημένου (*Eph.* xii. 2), which is common in this sense in Acts, nowhere else in the N.T.; *Smyrn.* iii. 3 = Acts x. 41. It is doubtful whether Ignatius knew the O.T., except through a book of Testimonia; he is steeped in a New Testament of which Acts is part.

[2] Cf. *Some Hellenistic Elements in Primitive Christianity*, p. 14, and add to the instances quoted Ptolemy Euergetes II in Jacoby, *F.G.H.* 234 F. 1 ff.; and see Jacoby's note *ad loc.* Cf. also p. 54, n. 1, below.

[3] Cf. Creed, *The Gospel according to St Luke*, Introd. p. xiii. The obvious candidate would be Titus, who figures prominently in the Epistles, but is never mentioned in Acts. His silence as to the events of Gal. ii would be easily explained.

(*The Acts of the Apostles*, Oxford 1933) on the ground of the numerous differences in the use of 'particles, prepositions, conjunctions and other small parts of speech' and also of 'variations in the use of common words and the choice between synonyms. Especial attention should be given to archaic idioms which tended to pass out of use in the koine, but survived in elegant writers.' Now there is no doubt that the tests in question, if rightly applied, are the really decisive ones. A writer may adopt or develop new theological views; in controversial literature, such as the Pauline Epistles, he may at different times be inconsistent: he may change his theological vocabulary as the language of theology develops; but normally his way of expressing himself will remain the same, provided that his style is not dislocated by a violent emotional upheaval or a deliberate attempt at fine writing. This is especially true of the Greek language, a language particularly rich in particles which enable a skilled writer to express various shades of meaning with great facility, while a bad writer fails to use them or uses them unskilfully. It may seem that to discuss such matters is to waste time over minute trivialities; but a man can be hanged for a finger-print. The importance of the question lies in the fact that if the Gospel and Acts were not written by the same author we have to allow that either the author or a very early editor of Acts added the introduction with intent to deceive, and suspicion is thrown on the whole book; on the other hand if they come from the same hand we have a very clear view of the tradition of the Gospel narrative current in the early Pauline Churches and of the history of the early years of the Church as it was viewed in those Churches. The investigation has the further advantage that it will throw a very clear light on the structure of the book of Acts itself.

But we must begin by noting what we mean when we say that a book in the ancient world was 'written' by 'an author'.

The normal method of writing history in the hellenistic era was not, as it is in modern times, to make exhaustive personal enquiries of eyewitnesses of contemporary events, to read the pamphlet literature of the past, if it could be found, and to examine the public documents and archaeological remains of the past and on the basis of these and similar enquiries to compile your narrative. A few of the greater historians sometimes went to the trouble of writing history in this kind of way: of those whose works have survived, Thucydides and Polybius stand alone in this respect. But the normal method was much simpler. You took the works of your predecessors in the same field, perhaps using any official lists and chronicles which were accessible, and used scissors and paste to make them into a consecutive whole, following the story which appealed to you as most probable or which suited best your political bias or your sense of dramatic fitness. Naturally you also falsified or distorted their narrative to suit your own ends. As a rule you also rewrote them in a more or less harmonious style, in accordance with the style of rhetoric which you favoured: history was after all a rhetorical exercise. There are many ancient writers whom we know to have been largely or mainly compilers of the work of their predecessors; but as a rule we cannot point with any certainty to stylistic peculiarities which prove that at this or that point an author is simply incorporating such and such a predecessor.[1] With the New Testament writers

[1] There are of course exceptions, cf. Norden, *Die Antike Kunstprosa*, p. 154, n. 1 (Posidonius and Strabo). In Philo, whose work is for the most part marked by an uniform dulness, the passage *Leg. ad G*. 81 ff. shows a remarkable lapse into the style of the diatribe, and an equally marked assumption of the real existence of the gods of the Greek pantheon; Philo is incorporating a pagan diatribe. A little later (145 ff.) we have a passage in the οὗτός ἐστιν ὁ style which is quite unlike the rest of Philo. But as a rule it is very hard to trace any obvious differences; yet Philo is from first to last a compiler of other men's treatises, lectures

we are in the fortunate position of having in St Mark's Gospel one of the sources used by two of his successors and being able to isolate another source or collection of smaller sources, the element known by theologians as 'Q'. (It may have been a single document, but it seems quite uncertain.) Now we are able to see fairly clearly what St Luke's method or lack of method as a compiler is from his dealings with Mark. On the whole he tries to effect what improvement he can in Mark's rather barbarous Greek, but it amounts to very little. Occasionally he inserts passages of really good Greek prose, but never for more than a sentence or two; his preface to his Gospel (i. 1–3) is the most notable instance, and we may add vii. 2–8, xvii. 20 and xxiii. 41.[1] He tries to get rid of barbarisms such as

? 27⁹¹

and sermons. For Thucydides among ancient historians cf. Seeck, *Entwicklung der antiken Geschichtschreibung*, pp. 68 ff.; for the influence of rhetoric on history, *ibid*. p. 89.

[1] For the first and last cf. *Hellenistic Elements*, p. 10 f. The first is important since it is a Lucan revision of a Q passage and shows that Luke's use of classical prose does not necessarily mean that he is inventing the passage. Thus the rejection of the logion xvii. 20 f. by Bultmann, *Gesch. d. synopt. Tradition* (cf. Dibelius, *From Tradition to Gospel*, p. 162), on the ground of the hellenic form, is quite unjustified; we have no reason to assume that Luke is not simply revising his source. His carelessness in revising his sources makes it difficult to form an accurate estimate of his ability as a writer of Greek. In Acts the we-sections are reasonably good, and in any case may represent no more than a diary kept at the time or written up soon afterwards. From the classical point of view the genitives absolute of xxi. 17 (with the redundant ἡμῶν... ἡμᾶς) and xxi. 34 are very bad. We have an atrocious heaping up of αὐτός and αὐτοί in xxii. 22–25; but is this Luke or a verbal reproduction of Paul's account of the scene? Unfortunately we have so little direct narrative in the Epistles that we cannot say how far he may have been in the habit of replacing the semitic suffix with a pronoun; Gal. i. 14 f. and 2 Cor. ii. 12 f. suggests that he may have done so; the rest of the narrative of Gal. i. 13–ii. 14 offers no means of judging. In xxviii. 8 ἐπιθεὶς τὰς χεῖρας αὐτῷ ἰάσατο αὐτόν (cf. Mark vi. 5, viii. 23) is bad,

5

Aramaic and Latin words with a moderate degree of success—but only a moderate degree. He reduces the thirty 'amens' of Matthew to six; but six remain.[1] At times he substitutes a properly constructed period for the semitic parataxis of Mark, but more often he lets it stand. The whole of his revision amounts to very little, and it is entirely without logical consistency. It is fairly easy to see why the revision is not more thorough; it may to some extent be due to Luke's own carelessness or pressure on his time, but the main reason seems to be that his sources, and the sources from which Mark and Q (if Q had been compiled into a single document) were composed, were collections of stories and sayings used in public worship by the Church and that only the most limited rewriting was possible if the hearers were not to be offended. Further the influence of the Greek Bible has actually led to the introduction of Hebraic Greek which is apparently intended to harmonise the Gospel with the language of the LXX; and it would seem that this introduction is in many cases at least to be ascribed to the evangelist himself, though here again there is a total lack of consistency. This appears in the characteristically Lucan phrase 'And it came to pass'. The words καὶ ἐγένετο may be followed either by another main verb, a pure Hebraism which is not Greek grammar at all, or by another main verb joined to ἐγένετο by καί, which is presumably grammatical, but shockingly bad style; or they may be followed by a subordinate clause in the infinitive, which, though still Hebraic, is

but conventional Christian Greek in describing a cure; otherwise these sections are distinctly superior to the rest of Acts. On the other hand Luke's ability as a writer of Greek should not be judged by his flashes of 'scholarship prose'. We have no reason to suppose that he could keep them up permanently.

[1] Cf. *Hellenistic Elements*, p. 8. After vi. 29 he omits the ἀγγαρεύσει μίλιον ἕν of Matt. v. 41 with its two barbarisms. He leaves 'Legion' and 'Beelzebub' but translates 'Talitha cumi'.

tolerable Greek. The first and worst of these occurs twenty-two times in the Gospel, never in Acts, the second eleven times in the Gospel, possibly once in Acts, the third and correct one five times in the Gospel and sixteen times in Acts. This looks fairly strong evidence for a difference of authorship, especially when we note that while eight instances of the worst use come from the infancy narrative and one from the story of the widow's son at Nain, where Luke is following very semitic sources, yet on the other hand in six cases it appears to represent a deliberate revision of Mark, who has nothing to correspond to the phrase. Similarly six cases of καὶ ἐγένετο καί represent deliberate revisions of Mark. On the other hand it must be noted that Clark has made an unaccountable mistake in saying that the first usage is peculiar to Luke; it appears five times in Matthew (vii. 28, xi. 1, xiii. 53, xix. 1 and xxvi. 1) in the hieratic formula with which Matthew concludes the great sections of his Gospel 'And it came to pass when Jesus had finished', before passing on to the next. Thus in this case, which is far the strongest that Clark produces, we must allow for the possibility that Luke has used a similar formula in order to give a hieratic ring to the Gospel. It must be remembered that though formally the Gospel is a work dedicated to Theophilus for his private edification, it is at least probable that Luke intended from the first that it should be used for reading in the worship of the Church; on the other hand there is no reason to suppose that he intended that the Acts should be used for this purpose, for which quite large parts of it are singularly unsuited, as any one who follows the Anglican lectionary knows only too well. Thus we have to allow for the possibility that the offending usages are introduced as a deliberate Hebraism in order to produce a biblical ring. They are not Aramaisms,[1] so that there is no question of their having crept in by a slovenly

[1] Creed, op. cit. Introd. p. lxxix.

7

lapse into the semitisms of popular speech in reproducing Mark; nor is there any question that the writer of the Gospel has in general done what he can to effect a superficial improvement in the Greek of his sources.[1] Of course it is not to be supposed that his 'Hebraisms' are due to a knowledge of Hebrew; he is simply affecting the style of the Greek LXX.

Thus in this case the discrepancy between the usage of the Gospel and the Acts proves nothing. Before considering his other cases we must note that while Clark criticises those who lump the Gospel and the Acts together and describe them all as 'Lucan', he does not himself observe that Acts is by no means a single document written by a single author. Before we consider the language of Acts we must begin by observing that it falls into two main parts, the first dealing with the story of the Church at Jerusalem with Peter as its central figure, the second with Paul and his mission to the Gentile Churches. Roughly the second part begins with chapter xiii. But in neither case are we simply dealing with a single document entirely composed by Luke. In the first half of the book we have to distinguish between several sources, some of which at least show symptoms of being 'translation-Greek' which has followed an Aramaic original so closely that the meaning can only be found by retranslating it into Aramaic.[2] This presence of genuine Aramaisms, as against the 'secondary semitisms' of the kind to be found when a good writer of Greek is translating from a semitic language into good Greek or into Greek with a semitic colouring, is held by de Zwaan to apply to i. 6–v. 16 and ix. 31–xi. 18 (we may see reason to modify this view in respect at least of some part of this section). On the other hand we find a

[1] Norden, *op. cit.* pp. 482 ff.
[2] For the whole question cf. de Zwaan in *Beginnings of Christianity*, II, 44 ff. (cf. also p. 141). For a discussion of the cases which appear to be decisive, cf. below, p. 20.

number of 'secondary semitisms' in the rest of the first part of the book, while there are also a number, though not so many in the second half. Again the first half contains a section (ix. 1–30) which should count with the second half, being the introduction of St Paul on to the stage, while the speeches, as we shall see, may be separate documents or drawn from a different oral source.

Now we cannot at the moment go fully into the question of the sources, but it is important to notice that the author's method of dealing with the material at his disposal corresponds very closely to that employed by Luke in writing the Gospel. We find a certain attempt to impose a superficial hellenism on semitic sources, or sources written in very semitic Greek. We find further another characteristic of the Gospel in the introduction of fragments of 'scholarship prose' into a narrative which in general is content with a far more pedestrian level, such as the preface, Philip's question to the Ethiopian eunuch and the answer (viii. 31–34) and elsewhere.[1] This latter characteristic is so peculiar as to make it extremely doubtful whether we can really separate at least the final reviser of the Gospel from the final reviser of the Acts. Still we cannot deny the possibility that two different compilers might have hit on the same idea of introducing a few sentences to create a favourable impression on Greek readers. On the other hand the fact that in both books we have a very superficial revision of written or oral sources means that we cannot just apply statistical methods, such as the counting of particles to the two books; we must distinguish between the stylistic peculiarities of the sources on the one hand and the stylistic peculiarities, if any, which we can ascribe to the compiler on the other. We must bear in mind the point we have already noted, that the Gospel had to be more suited to liturgical needs. And we must also

[1] Cf. *Hellenistic Elements*, p. 16.

allow for the possibility that the same writer may vary a good deal from day to day. Clark's two test cases μέν and τε, if strictly applied, would have the result of proving that Romans and Galatians do not come from the pen of the same writer, since in Romans we find μέν nineteen times (two being doubtful) and τε sixteen times, while the figures for Galatians are three (one doubtful) and nil. No doubt Luke was not so temperamental as Paul; but it probably needed a conscious effort if Luke was to write Greek that rose above the level of fair average koine.

With these considerations in mind we may turn to Clark's results. The difference on which he lays most emphasis, (pp. 396 f.), is in the use of the particles μέν and τε. On his calculation, μέν appears eleven times in the Gospel and fifty-one times in Acts, μέν by itself being used once in the Gospel as against fifteen times in Acts and μὲν οὖν once in the Gospel against twenty-seven times in Acts. This looks a formidable difference. But if we look more closely we find that Luke has introduced μέν six times in revising his sources or in passages where he is writing independently, in addition to the four times where he found it in his sources (I can only find ten occasions of the use of the word in Moulton and Geden's *Concordance*). In Acts μέν appears once in the preface. From Acts i. 5 to the end of xii it appears sixteen times; in the rest of the book it appears thirty-one times (again Moulton and Geden give a total of forty-eight). Here we either have to argue that Acts comes from two different authors or else to recognise that there is no significant difference between the Gospel and the first half of Acts, especially when we notice that μὲν οὖν only occurs nine times in the first half of Acts and that five of these are in editorial summaries some of which may be inserted by Luke, as against eighteen times in the last part.

The case of τε looks even stronger, since it appears 158 times in Acts (allowing for several dubious readings) as against eight times in Luke. Yet here we must be warned by the fact that in four cases we are dealing with passages peculiar to Luke and in the other four with alterations (twice of Mark and twice of Q), so that it looks as though Luke, if left to himself, would have used it more freely.[1] Again of the cases in Acts only forty-seven out of 158 fall in Acts i–xii. Of these forty-seven, three fall into the catalogue of nations in ii. 9–11, where the use of τε καί was so obvious that the source, which Luke was using for these verses, could hardly fail to introduce it. Five fall in the section ii. 37–47; seven (one doubtful) in chap. viii and six in ix. 1–30, a hellenistic, perhaps Antiochene source dealing with the conversion of St Paul; we find none in the very semitic 'Acts of Peter' with which the chapter ends. The other two passages ii. 37–47 and chap. viii may simply owe the frequency of τε to greater care in revision on the part of the compiler; in any case in the remainder of the first twelve chapters of Acts the particle only appears twenty-six times. I doubt if we can attach any weight to the apparent preponderance of τε in Acts as against Luke; the phenomena seem to me to point rather to the same very slovenly reviser and to a certain hesitation about revising his sources for the Gospel.

His next instance is the preference of the more classical σύν to μετά in Acts. The Gospel expresses 'with' by μετά and the genitive fifty-two times as against Acts' thirty-seven times; by σύν twenty-six times as against Acts' fifty-one times. I am not at all clear that the difference is large enough to be significant at the best of times, even if we take Moulton and Geden's figure of twenty-four for the Gospel. Quite clearly it becomes insignificant when we note that of Luke's twenty-four uses of

---

[1] Clark wrongly states that all cases in Luke are of 'the τε καί type which lingered on in the koine after the τε and the τε...τε types fell out of use.' This appears not to be the case in Luke xxiv. 20.

σύν, no fewer than fourteen are in passages peculiar to him;[1] six are revisions of Mark, two of Q, the other two were already given by the sources. We may note as a curiosity that at ix. 4 he has changed Mark's σύν to μετά; but quite clearly his general tendency is to use σύν more often than his sources. It must of course be remembered that both forms were perfectly good Greek by any standards. On the other hand we find that in Acts, out of fifty-three times where σύν appears, thirty-three fall in the second half as against twenty in the first,[2] so that here again Luke's usage is largely determined by that of the sources which he revises so superficially. Even so we find μετά twenty-two times in the second half of Acts as against fourteen times in the first. Here then we can draw no inferences.

At first sight there is a better case in the uses of the two words ἀνήρ and ἄνθρωπος in the two books. Properly ἀνήρ is a human being of the male sex, ἄνθρωπος simply a human being; it can be used in the feminine. Luke uses ἀνήρ twenty-seven times, Acts 101; ἄνθρωπος 100 times as against Acts' forty-six. But these figures need heavy qualification. It is a small point that Luke happens to use ἀνήρ in the sense of 'husband' or of 'men' as against women, where the word

---

[1] Classification is not always easy, e.g. vii. 6 where Luke has largely rewritten Q for the reasons noted in *Hellenistic Elements*, p. 10. Where however the pericope as a whole comes from Mark or Q I have counted the alteration as a revision. The argument is not affected in either case. It must not be supposed that the greater frequency of Lucan language in passages peculiar to himself is due to the fact that they were invented by him; if he was aware that a passage, which came to him on what he, rightly or wrongly, regarded as good authority, had not hitherto appeared in any Greek version of the Gospel, he would naturally feel free to improve the Greek, if he was not himself translating from the Aramaic.

[2] Moulton and Geden give fifty-three as against fifty-one, two cases (one in each half) being doubtful.

could not be avoided, five times, while Acts happens to use it in this way nine times. On the other hand it is not a small point that of the times when ἄνθρωπος appears in Luke no fewer than twenty-four are in the technical term ὁ υἱὸς τοῦ ἀνθρώπου 'the Son of Man', a term which obviously could not be altered; as it happens the phrase only appears once in Acts. And again of the times when ἀνήρ is used in Acts twenty-nine are such phrases as 'Men and brethren' or 'Men of Israel' at the opening or in the course of one of the set speeches which form so large a part of the book. We can hardly imagine the most ardent Hellenist opening the Sermon on the Mount, the Little Apocalypse or one of the Matthean discourses by putting such phrases in the mouth of Jesus; so we must rewrite Clark's figures by allowing for these inevitable differences. The result is that we get

| ἀνήρ | Luke 22. | Acts 64. |
| ἄνθρωπος | Luke 76. | Acts 44. |

The result is a good deal less significant, and in the second case quite negligible, especially when we note that ἄνθρωπος in Luke is often used correctly; he uses ἄνθρωπος for the "men" who build their houses on the rock and on the sand respectively as against the ἀνήρ of Matthew. At least thirty of the cases in which he uses the word are strictly correct since they apply to all mankind as such, as in the Golden Rule, 'Whatsoever ye would that men should do unto you'. None the less, Acts shows a considerable preponderance in its use of ἀνήρ, though it is by no means consistent. In some cases its use of ἄνθρωπος may be justified by a certain note of contempt, as in v. 28 ('to bring this man's blood upon us'), but this does not apply to the speech of Gamaliel. On the other hand while its use of ἀνήρ is fairly equally divided between the two main divisions of the book, in the first half it is curiously uneven. Of the thirty-eight times where it appears in this half nine are in openings of speeches, while in five it is used in contrast with women or in the sense of husband. Of the remaining twenty-four no less than twelve occur in the section ix. 32–x. 48 describing Peter's miracles in Palestine and the conversion of Cornelius. This section is remarkable, since in at least one passage it is scarcely intelligible except as a mistranslation of an Aramaic original; yet it is also peculiarly rich in Lucan words and idioms; we shall deal with it later.[1] For our present purpose it is enough to notice that outside this one section the uses of ἀνήρ in the first half of Acts, apart from the cases which have been noticed, are reduced to twelve.[2]

The facts as to the variations in language would indeed prove, if they proved anything at all, that the first half of Acts was written by the author of the Gospel (or at any rate that there is no reason why they should not have been written by the same author), while the second half was added by another hand. We could even strengthen the argument by pointing out that the rather semitic ἰδού appears fifty-five times in the Gospel, sixteen times in the first half of Acts and only seven times in the second, in all cases but one being in reported utterances of St Paul.[3] On the other hand we have to face the fact that in the Gospel we are dealing with a very careless reviser, and that exactly the same phenomenon meets us in Acts. The result is that Clark's linguistic researches, whatever their value in drawing attention to the unevenness of the reviser's methods may be, tend to prove that the same hand is responsible for the final compilation both of the Acts and the Gospel. It is only reasonable to suppose that it is the same hand that has added the two prefaces and the incidental pieces of 'scholarship prose'

[1] See below, p. 32.
[2] For a discussion of the rest of Clark's instances of differences of language and idioms between the Gospel and the Acts, cf. Appendix.
[3] *Hellenistic Elements*, p. 17, n. 2.

and that it is the hand of the writer of the 'we-sections'. There seems no reason to doubt that it is the hand of Luke 'the beloved physician'. Whether or no the Acts shows special evidence of medical knowledge and interests may be doubtful; if we admit these points, further enquiry as to the author would only land us in the position of the schoolboy who was being introduced to the Homeric question and said that so far as he could see it had been established that Homer wasn't written by Homer but by another man with the same name.

CHAPTER II

THE SOURCES OF ACTS

We may now consider the material which Luke had at his disposal for compiling his history of the early days of the Church. Here I would begin with a caution. In the early decades of the present century splitting the Acts was almost as popular a pastime with the critics as splitting the atom with the scientists in the present decade. Now undoubtedly Acts is a composite document, in which 'sources' of some kind have been used, which simply means that except for the 'we-sections' the author did not invent it out of his own head. But was he using written sources or was he taking down the reminiscences of those who could give him information? And further does he, as he does in the Gospel, reproduce his sources in continual blocks from a written original, with very slight revision, or does he feel at liberty to reconstruct them by combining material from his various sources into a composite whole? And in this composite whole, are parts derived from oral and part from written sources? And can we really distinguish between a written and an oral source at all, except where we have, as in the case of the Gospels, the written source employed by both evangelists in Mark, and the large amount of material used by both in Q, where the verbal agreements and the impossibility of supposing that one was copying the other make the assumption of a written source almost, if not quite, inevitable?[1]

[1] I am not here concerned to deny that some or perhaps all of the material known as Q existed independently in a written form of some kind; but I am not at all clear how one can be entirely certain in distinguishing between a written source and an oral source committed to memory in a fixed form for purposes of liturgical usage. Nor is it clear

In considering these questions we must begin by noting the
enormous change of outlook on these questions which follows
from Professor Dodd's work, *The Apostolic Preaching and its
Developments*. It seems to me that he has completely made out
his case for supposing that the speeches ascribed to Peter in the
first half of Acts 'represent, not indeed what Peter said upon
this or that occasion, but the kerygma of the Church at Jerusalem at an early period' (*op. cit.* p. 37). This kerygma was
itself based on a Jewish model; for a recitation of God's mighty
works in the history of Israel was a recognised method of
argument, preaching and teaching as far back at least as the
book of Deuteronomy, where we find a formula to be recited
at the offering of the first-fruits by the worshipper in which
these mighty acts are recited in a summary form, replacing no
doubt some highly syncretistic act of oblation derived from
the worship of the Baalim of Canaan.[1] In Acts we have several
speeches of this type ascribed to Peter, and Paul. They open
with an appeal to prophecy or history, varying with the point
which the speaker wished to prove.[2] This leads up to the
appearance of Jesus, preceded by John the Baptist, His death,
as part of the divine plan, His resurrection and exaltation, the

whether information given by word of mouth can be distinguished from
information given, for example, by letter: one is 'oral' and one is
'written', but it is hard to see.what difference there is between them in
reliability. In what follows I use 'oral' of any traditions that had not
been committed to writing before they came to Luke or at least assumed
a fixed oral form for liturgical or catechetical purposes.

[1] Deut. xxvi. 5 ff.; for a very verbose version see Neh. ix. For the
whole subject cf. *Gentiles*, pp. 27 ff. To the parallels quoted there
should be added the liturgy of the Apostolic Constitutions VII, xxxiii,
1 ff. (originally Jewish).

[2] An amusing point emerges at Acts xiii. 21, where Paul drags in an
apparently irrelevant reference to 'Saul the son of Kish'. Was it a
rabbinical practice to introduce a panegyric of your eponymous hero
from the Old Testament where you could?

sending of the Holy Spirit and the future coming of the Lord in Glory; the message ends with a call to repentance. There are variations in the speeches; the whole scheme of salvation is not necessarily set out in all of them. There is a particularly significant item in the longest of Peter's speeches in Acts x. 34 ff., where in verse 38 we have a summary of the synoptic Gospel story, and another at the end of Paul's speech in Acts xiii. 38 ff., where we have a summary of Paul's teaching on justification attached to his version. It looks as though Luke was aware of individual variations in the emphasis laid by the two Apostles on different aspects of the Gospel. But it remains true that what we have is a summary of a more or less established form of missionary preaching, based on a more or less fixed scheme and known to Luke in various forms (possibly those of Jerusalem and Antioch). But this statement of the Gospel is really independent of his narrative and is introduced by him at what he regards as suitable points. The result is that in trying to find the nature of his source for any particular incident, we must rule out the speeches entirely, since they have no real connection with their context.

With this caution we may consider the various sections of Acts. Torrey's search for Aramaisms and translation Greek (*Composition and Date of Acts*, Harvard Theological Studies, vol. 1) may be held to have established his case so far as Acts i.–v. 16 are concerned, except for the opening clause. The very clumsy opening of i. 1, where we suddenly break off from a stylish Greek preface into a rather semitic narrative of the Ascension which contradicts the ending of the Gospel, is quite easily explained if we suppose that Luke had a source before him which he considered not less worthy of credence than that which formed the close of the Gospel.[1]

[1] A similar conflation of sources by Mark appears to be the explanation of the two 'trials' of Jesus before the Sanhedrin in Mark xiv. 55 ff. and

But have we here a single source, or two? Harnack, followed by the editors of *The Beginnings of Christianity*,[1] would sub-divide this section into two sources, the story of Pentecost, the arrest of 'the Apostles', their miraculous liberation, trial and final dismissal being treated as a doublet of the other narrative; this other narrative recorded the healing of the lame man in the Temple, the trial before the Sanhedrin and release of Peter and John and an outpouring of the Holy Spirit, which Harnack takes as the original and less miraculous story of Pentecost. Now here we must be careful to distinguish between two entirely different questions. One question is whether the two stories which Harnack distinguishes are really duplicate versions of the same history. The other is whether Luke had before him two narratives of the same set of events which he combined just as he and Matthew combined Mark and Q, except for the fact that Mark and Q contained very few duplicates. Harnack holds that Luke simply combined two sources. It seems to me that this is a very difficult view to maintain for the following reasons:

(1) Torrey in arguing for an Aramaic original of the first fifteen chapters of Acts is generally held not to have made out

xv. 1. Mark had a source which described the proceedings and another which simply stated that there had been some kind of a meeting of the Sanhedrin as a result of which Jesus was accused before Pilate. He simply included both, to the infinite puzzlement of critics. The difference in the account of Luke xxiv. 51 (where καὶ ἀνεφέρετο εἰς τὸν οὐρανόν is an obvious attempt to harmonize the two stories) is remarkable. But it is quite possible that Luke only came across his Ascension story some time after the completion of the Gospel; we have no evidence that he composed Acts quite soon after. On the other hand it is quite possible that he found it in a different stratum of tradition and included it without asking questions as to the contradiction of the two stories.

[1] Harnack, *The Acts of the Apostles*, pp. 179 ff.; *Beginnings of Christianity*, II, 139 ff.

2-2

his case as a whole. But it is generally agreed that in the section we are considering he has established his point.[1] Thus ii. 47 'The Lord added daily those that were being saved together' is meaningless as Greek; but it can represent an Aramaic original with a slightly different pointing which would mean 'The Lord added those who were being saved exceedingly' or as we should put it 'on a large scale' or 'in great numbers'. In iii. 16 the text runs 'In the faith in His name, His name hath strengthened this man whom ye see and know and the faith which is through Him hath given him this health'. This is meaningless; but it can be translated into an Aramaic which means 'And by faith in His name he hath made strong this man whom ye see and know; yea, faith which is through Him hath given him this health'. Here we have a perfectly good sense. Yet again in iv. 24 ff. we have a hopeless jumble of words and no plausible method of amending the Greek; but by assuming an Aramaic original which had changed a *yod* into a *vau*, a trifling and common corruption, we get the meaning 'Master, who madest heaven and earth and sea and all that is in them, that which (or as we should say 'as') our father David said by the mouth of the Holy Spirit', which is perfectly reasonable. Now it seems to me extraordinarily difficult to suppose that in this section we have two original Aramaic documents, both affected by similar mistranslations. It must be remembered that Peter's speech on the day of Pentecost is an inserted kerygma, while that of Gamaliel in v. 35–39 is probably Luke's own composition; the speech of Peter in iii. 13–26, is a short kerygma, with some testimonia appended, which probably had an independent existence: Peter's speeches before the Sanhedrin in iv. 9–14 and 19 f. are again probably Lucan. This leaves us

[1] *Op. cit.* pp. 14 ff. His findings for this section are accepted by de Zwaan in *Beginnings of Christianity*, II, 50 ff. Cf. Dodd, *Apostolic Preaching*, p. 35.

two very short documents, which are hardly likely to have had an independent existence.

(2) The numbers of those converted (3,000 on the day of Pentecost, rising to 5,000 by Acts iv. 4) present an almost insuperable difficulty; two Aramaic sources which could limit themselves to such modest figures are unthinkable in view of the type of exaggeration in which Josephus habitually indulges.[1]

(3) We have no explanation of the origin or preservation of such documents; they cannot be explained, like the materials which lie behind Mark, as short collections of miracles or sayings of Jesus compiled and preserved for homiletic purposes.

Thus it seems far more likely that Luke has collected from one or more informants all the materials he could; the informants spoke Aramaic and Luke or his agent translated them inaccurately, so that the inaccuracies appear in Peter's kerygma and also in both of the two accounts which Harnack regards as duplicates. We have no reason to suppose that there was any Church history before Luke and it seems likely that for the most part he had to collect his own material from the available oral reminiscences of the Christians of Jerusalem. It is of course possible that he has in all good faith inserted duplicate accounts of the same incident; the two trials before the Sanhedrin have the air of doublets. On the other hand while it is possible to hold that we have two accounts of the day of Pentecost there is not a scrap of evidence that this is so. We must remember that outpourings of the Holy Ghost were of frequent occurrence in the primitive Church as the Pauline Epistles show, and Harnack's attempt to reduce the number is purely due to his distrust of the miraculous, which may or may not be well-founded, but was certainly not shared by the primi-

[1] E.g. *B.J.* ii, 280 (3,000,000 Jews meet Cestius Gallus to protest against Florus), *Antt.* xx, 112 (20,000 killed in a riot in the time of Cumanus's procuratorship).

tive Church. In a Church which believes that miraculous speaking with tongues is likely to happen, it is likely to happen frequently.

This oral account has probably been expanded by Luke with some, though not all of his summaries; the summary of ii. 41 ff. contains one of the Aramaisms we have noted. On the other hand the summary of iv. 32 seems intended to introduce Barnabas[1] and the story of Ananias and Sapphira, which looks like a miracle-story preserved in the tradition of the Church as the miracle-stories of the Gospel were; we shall find other specimens later. The application of the methods of form-criticism to the Gospels has thrown a flood of light on the earlier history of their materials, and it may well be that the impressive, if unedifying, story of Ananias and his wife was preserved simply as a miracle-story; we may note that it ends with a substitute for the typical acclamation.

Before leaving this section of Acts we may glance at the notorious difficulty of the speech of Gamaliel, in which Theudas precedes Judas of Galilee as a Jewish rebel.[2] Josephus quite definitely represents Judas as the first rebel, and as he is following Nicolas of Damascus here, he is probably right;

---

[1] Torrey (*op. cit.* p. 31) suggests that μεθερμηνευόμενον means 'being interpreted euphemistically'. He holds that Barnabas = 'Bar-Nebo', Nebo being a demon, presumably the Babylonian god degraded to that position. Such euphemistic interpretations were common in Judaism. This seems highly unlikely; the name is said to have been conferred by the Apostles, who would not have given their benefactor so undesirable a name; we have no reason to suppose that he had ever been a persecutor like Saul, who might have been given such a name. For its meaning cf. *Beginnings of Christianity*, IV, 49. Torrey claims that in v. 7 ἐγένετο δὲ ὡς ὡρῶν τριῶν διάστημα καί is typical translation Greek, but the phrase is a natural variation of the ἐγένετο δὲ...καί followed by a main verb common in Luke's Gospel.

[2] *Antt.* XX, 97 and 102; cf. Schürer, *G.J.V.* I, 566.

in general he is the most unreliable and mendacious of writers. On the other hand Josephus describes the rebellion of Theudas as falling under Fadus (A.D. 44), after the supposed date of this speech; immediately afterwards he describes a revolt started by the grandsons of Judas. It has been held that Luke is simply following Josephus carelessly at this point, and therefore that Acts must be dated after the publication of the *Antiquities* in A.D. 93. The suggestion has been made (Streeter, *The Four Gospels*, pp. 557f.) that Luke heard Josephus lecture in Rome; this may be correct, but it is at least as likely that Luke took his information from the same source as Josephus and reproduced it less correctly. In any case the speech is not to be taken as a report, or even a summary of what Gamaliel said. But the inaccuracies do not prove that Luke is not correct in his record of the fact which the speech implies, namely that the Pharisees, led by Gamaliel, refused to continue the policy of persecution on the ground that Christianity was not a political movement, and that in religion it stood for much that the Pharisees held, as against the Sadducees.

With Acts vi we come to a new stratum dealing with the story of Stephen. Here again we must separate the speech from the story as a whole. The speech of Stephen, apart from its Lucan introduction and conclusion, is a kerygma of the Old Testament, which is concerned to point out that from the beginning the Jews have misunderstood their religion; it is the theme of the Epistle of Barnabas and is here advanced in a document so skilfully constructed that Harnack (*Acts*, p. 173) supposes that it has been softened down, since 'while its depreciatory attitude towards the Temple is still clearly recognisable, its attitude towards the Law is quite obscure'. Exactly what more definite condemnation of the Law was needed than to say that Israel in the desert rejected the 'living oracles' originally given and made a Golden Calf, and were in consequence left to serve the host of heaven does not appear.[1] In view of its quite non-Pauline character it is not likely to be Luke's own compilation, and he would hardly have been guilty of such barbarous Greek; the conclusion, which seems to be his work, is of entirely different calibre.[2] This leaves us with a difficulty. The story of Stephen proceeds quite smoothly down to the end of chap. vi; but after it we have what looks suspiciously like a double story of his martyrdom in vii. 54–58 and 59 f. Harnack suggests (p. 173) that the former of these containing a trial and the speech comes from one source, while the latter, which is the true one, describes his lynching by the Hellenists of the synagogue. It is urged in support of this that the Sanhedrin had no power to inflict a death-penalty.

The last point is undoubtedly true, but the last decades before the fall of Jerusalem offer many examples of illegalities and the interval between the dismissal of Pilate and the arrival of his successor offered a moment when the High Priest could easily have justified his action.[3]

The objection to the view that we have two sources con-

---

[1] For the whole speech cf. *Jerusalem*, pp. 43 ff.; for the view that we have here an ancient Hellenistic-Jewish document in which the Torah is definitely rejected, cf. Foakes Jackson in Moffatt's commentary on Acts. It may represent a good tradition of what Stephen held, since he may quite well have been the originator of this attitude to the Law, which is quite different from that of St Paul. It appears in the Preaching of Peter, (Clem. Alex. *Strom.* VI, v. 41, (760P) and Orig. *In Jo.* XIII, xvii. 104 (IV. 241)), where the Jews worship angels and the month and the moon. It may represent a misinterpretation of the Pauline view (Gal. iv. 3 and 10, cf. *Gentiles*, pp. 104 ff.) that the Torah is powerless to save man from the power of the celestial bodies which determine the fate of man, but it is radically different from it. On the other hand it is quite possible that Stephen was capable of arriving at such a system for himself. For the view cf. also Justin *Dial.* 19 (237A).

[2] Cf. *Hellenistic Elements*, pp. 14 f.

[3] Cf. *Jerusalem*, loc. cit.

flated by Luke is that there is no obvious point in the story of chap. vi at which the conflation begins; moreover, if we are right in holding that the speech was originally an independent document in the form of a pamphlet against orthodox Judaism, both stories would be far too short to have existed as independent documents; even if we suppose that one of them was the opening of a fuller narrative which goes on to describe the mission of the Hellenists at Antioch and the other an account of the missionary activity of Philip, we have two very short documents; and again we have no reason to suppose that the Church was interested to write its own history or to compile its own hagiology. The probable explanation of the doublets is that Luke found both stories current and recorded them both.[1]

The Philip stories seem however to come from a different stratum; Harnack is probably right in holding that xi. 19 resumes from viii. 4 the story of the means by which the Gospel reached Antioch. Philip's visit to Sebaste (or to an unspecified city in Samaria) has given rise to a host of theories which are quite without foundation in the story itself. Philip goes to Samaria and there converts a number of Samaritans including a local pseudo-Messiah named Simon, described by his followers (and presumably by himself) as 'the great Power of God' or 'the Greatness', a title modelled on the Jewish use of the Gebhurah as a periphrasis for the name of Jahweh.[2] The mission

[1] It is suggested (*Beginnings of Christianity*, II, 150) that the original lynching story consisted of vi. 8–11 and vii. 54–58a. But there must have been more detail as to the dragging of Stephen out of the city, and there is no need to regard 11 and 12 ff. as doublets; the first verse describes the raising of the outcry, the latter its results. Harnack's objection to the 'false' witnesses (p. 172) is a genuine literary curiosity; any witness who gives evidence against a martyr must be a 'false' witness since he is against the truth.

[2] Cf. *Beginnings of Christianity*, IV, 91. The awkward term indicates Luke's failure to understand the term; we have a similar misunderstanding

of Peter and John is natural, since it was at the moment uncertain how far the Gospel could be preached to those who were
not Jews; the attempt of Simon to buy the power to convey
the gift of the Holy Ghost is natural in a society where religion
and magic are as near to one another as they were on the fringes
of Judaism in the hellenistic age. All this section looks as
though it were based on oral reminiscences of Philip himself.[1]

With chap. ix we resume the story of Saul, introduced by
viii. 3. The story of Paul's conversion in Acts is one of the
main difficulties of the book. The difficulty is not that there are
minor discrepancies of detail; Paul may well have varied his
account in regard to such points, and Luke may simply be
reproducing the variations he has heard.[2] The natural expla-

in Luke xxii. 69. Torrey's suggestion of an Aramaic original 'the power
of the God who is called Great' is unnecessary. Even if we read τὴν
πόλιν and take it to mean Sebaste, we cannot use Wellhausen's statement
that Sebaste was never Jewish but remained heathen to mean that there
were no Jews there; if Philip had really preached to the local heathen, the
question of circumcision must have been raised at once. On the view
that Simon was a pseudo-Messiah it is fitting that Philip should preach
about the kingdom of God. But the term, though rare in Acts, can be
used quite conventionally as in xiv. 22 and xx. 25.

[1] The whole of the Philip section is fairly free from semitisms, which
is natural if Luke derived his information from Philip, who was a
'Hellenist', i.e. a Jew of the Dispersion who had settled in Jerusalem.
For the scholarship-prose and the testimonium in viii. 31 ff., and the
suspicion that we have a visionary experience of Philip which has become
a historical incident cf. *Hellenistic Elements*, p. 16.

[2] Thus xxii. 9 contradicts ix. 7 as to the hearing of the voice by Paul's
companions, xxvi. 14 represents his companions as falling to the ground,
while in ix. 7 they stand speechless. Similarly the command to preach to
the Gentiles comes in ix. 15 to Ananias, and is presumably handed on by
him to Paul; in xxii. 17 ff. it comes in a special vision in the Temple; in
xxvi. 16 ff. it is given in the vision on the road to Damascus. But the
vision in the Temple may well have repeated the original command;
nothing is gained by trying to reduce the number of Paul's visions, which

nation would be that they come from different sources; but once again we are faced with what seems an insuperable difficulty in imagining the kind of source which would record the incident. I cannot believe in a kind of chronicle or minute-book of the Church of Jerusalem or Antioch, still less in a chronicle which would record the story of Paul's conversion in this detailed way.[1] The problem is not the discrepancies, but the repetition; it is inevitable that we should have the story in its proper historical place, perhaps tolerable that we should have one account of it in Paul's defence of himself; but two repetitions in the two speeches to the Jews and to Festus are very bad writing. On the other hand the repetition is entirely deliberate. For the two speeches demonstrate the fact that Paul's conception of the Gospel, carrying with it the mission to the Gentiles without the imposition on them of the observance of the Torah, is 'to the Jews a stumbling-block and to the Greeks foolishness'. In xxii. 3–21 everything leads up to the vision charging Paul to leave Jerusalem to preach to the Gentiles; it is at this point that he is shouted down. In xxvi. 4–23 the series of testimonies, whose quotation is implied in Festus's interruption, has been cut out in order to emphasise the fact that Christ, the new 'light of the world' is to be preached to Gentiles as well as to Jews. Here we have Paul's own conception of the Gospel as a world-religion, not as a mere sect of Judaism. According to Paul himself (Gal. i. 6)

were obviously frequent (cf. 2 Cor. xii. 1 ff.). In xxvi. 16 ff. the compression of the story has eliminated Ananias entirely.

[1] The suggestion that Acts ix. may represent the Jerusalem version of the story (*Beginnings of Christianity*, II, 153) seems peculiarly unlikely. It is argued that the story of Ananias is the kind of story against which Paul protests in Gal. i. 1. But in ix. 17 f. Ananias is only the minister of baptism, which carries with it the normal gift of the Spirit; in xxii. 15 Ananias tells Paul that he is to be witness to Christ before all men. Here, if anywhere, is his Apostolic commission.

any other conception is a 'different Gospel'.[1] Now Paul was right in this view, and Luke is right in emphasising the importance he attaches to it; but it is very clumsy, and very semitic to add emphasis to a point by mere repetition; Luke could easily have given a summary, at least in xxvi. 4 ff.[2] On the other hand the use of this clumsy method may not be entirely due to Luke's incompetence; he was writing for a public which was largely semitic, and he may have known that it was the best means of driving home his point.[3]

The story of Paul's conversion is continued in the summary which describes Paul's mission to the Jews of Damascus, their attempt to kill him and his escape, his acceptance by the Church as a disciple, his mission to the Hellenists and his departure for Tarsus. The same ground is covered by Gal. i. 17–19 and 2 Cor. xi. 32 f. There are several notorious discrepancies so far as the Galatian story is concerned. The omission of Paul's visit to Arabia is unimportant, since Luke is not concerned to give a detailed itinerary. Nor can we press the fact that Paul claims that he saw none of the Apostles but 'Cephas' and James the Lord's brother as against the account in Acts of his introduction

---

[1] The point, to which may be added the statement of the commands of the vision in terms of later Pauline theology (for Acts xxvi. 18 cf. Col. i. 13), indicate that Luke knew more of Paul's epistles, or at least of his habitual teaching, than is sometimes allowed. Festus's interruption at xxvi. 24 may well be a genuine historical reminiscence, since it is the kind of detail that would be remembered. Moreover, it does not fit the text as it stands; Paul has not introduced πολλὰ γράμματα except by implication. But if we realise that xxvi. 23 is a summary of a long roll of testimonies (which Luke has probably inserted elsewhere), the interruption becomes intelligible.

[2] For repetition as a clumsy and semitic way of emphasising a point cf. de Zwaan in H.T.R. XVII, ii. 116.

[3] Theophilus may or may not have been a Jew; Josephus mentions two Jews of that name. But his public in the early Church was bound to be very largely Jewish.

to 'the Apostles' by Barnabas; Barnabas was probably not regarded as an 'Apostle' at the time and the statement that he was introduced to 'the Apostles' need only be a loose way of saying that he was introduced to Peter and James. Nor need the plot of the Hellenist Jews against Paul's life (confirmed by xxii. 18) imply a longer residence than a fortnight on the occasion of this visit; Paul was quite capable of making Jerusalem too hot to hold him in a fortnight. On the other hand it must be admitted that the statement that he was with the Apostles 'going in and out of Jerusalem', i.e. associating on a footing of equality with them, can scarcely be harmonised with Galatians. It would seem that Luke did not know Galatians and found that when he came to write the story of Paul's career he had no very detailed information as to what precisely had happened, apart from such details as the plot of the Hellenists and the intervention of Barnabas. Hence he gives a summary representing what he supposes to have happened. As against this it must be noted that his story of the escape from Damascus agrees almost verbatim with 2 Cor. xi. 33 except that a rather more classical σπυρίς is substituted for the Pauline σαργάνη. Luke may have read the passage in 2 Cor.; but it is equally likely that he had often heard Paul 'glorying in his infirmities'.[1]

[1] Linguistic evidence supports the view that we are dealing with a Lucan editing of Paul's reminiscences and his own composition where the reminiscences failed. The only Aramaism noted by Torrey is 'the way' as a name for Christianity. But it appears here only in the first half of Acts, nine times, either simply or as 'the way of the Lord', etc. in the second half; elsewhere in the N.T. only in 2 Pet. (ii. 2, 15, 21). Several of the words which Clark regards as characteristic of Acts rather than the Gospel, while they are in fact characteristic of the second part of Acts as against the first, appear here; τε makes four out of forty-eight appearances in Acts i–xii in this section. The most significant point is that μαθητής is used absolutely of Christians twelve times in the first

The next section, ix. 32–43, is one of the most peculiar in Acts. The story of Aeneas is simply a miracle-story of the type familiar in the synoptic Gospels; we have the customary evidence as to the seriousness of the disease, the word of power which heals and the acclamation in the form of the conversion of all the inhabitants of Lydda and the Sharon plain. Tabitha is at first sight more fully told; but appearances are deceptive. Verses 38 f. are simply a Lucan insertion to bring Peter from Lydda to Joppa.[1] It would seem that the two incidents are drawn from a collection of miracles ascribed to Peter, but not cast into the form of a journey; there may have been a written collection of such miracles, since it is conceivable that such a collection might have been drawn up for apologetic purposes, but it is equally possible that we are dealing with oral tradition.[2]

half of Acts as against sixteen in the second; of these twelve appearances five are in the Antiochene narrative, vi. 1, 2, 7 and xi. 19–30; one is in the Lucan insertion, ix. 38 (cf. the following note); the remaining six all fall in this section, ix. 1–30. μαθήτρια in ix. 36 is probably a Lucan addition to his source, due to the frequent references to disciples in the foregoing sections. For this as a Lucan tendency cf. *Beginnings of Christianity*, IV, 91.

[1] Note the appearance of μαθηταί: the syntax of the verses is good, whereas in the rest of the story we have a paratactic arrangement with a few participles in the nominative substituted for main verbs as in verse 40.

[2] It would seem that we have isolated miracle-stories which have not yet lost their original details of place as have the majority of the Gospel stories (cf. Vincent Taylor, *Formation of the Gospel Tradition*, pp. 38 f.). Here we have stories which are still localised; hence Luke has to bring Peter from Lydda to Joppa. Originally it was not necessary to bring Peter to Lydda; the opening of verse 32 is simply Luke's explanation of how he came to be there. Torrey claims that διὰ πάντων represents an Aramaic original, but it may be simply a vague Lucan introduction implying that Peter was conducting a general visitation of the Church in Palestine. In ix. 31 he claims οἰκοδομουμένη καὶ πορευομένη as a semitism

On the other hand the story of Cornelius in chap. x is a narrative of a wholly different type, ix. 43 being simply an editorial link to keep Peter at Joppa; he may have stayed there between the two incidents (if we accept Tabitha as historical), but there is no reason to think that he did. We only know that in Luke's tradition both incidents were located there. The story is told on an entirely different scale and has none of the unities of time and place characteristic of popular tradition. The actual story of Cornelius must be distinguished from Peter's kerygma of the Gospel enshrined in it. This appears to be translated from an Aramaic original; Torrey points out that x. 36 can be translated back into Aramaic, which would mean 'As for the word which the Lord of all sent to the children of Israel, preaching peace through Jesus Christ, ye know the matter which took place in all Judaea'.[1] This gives excellent sense, while the text as it stands can hardly be translated without desperate emendations. But there is no reason to suppose that the sermon has any organic connection with its present context; it is simply a specimen of the primitive preaching included here because the occasion seemed suitable. On the other hand the first part of the Cornelius story (x. 1–33 and 44–48), though

similar to that of such passages as 2 Sam. iii. 1; but in that case οἰκοδο-μουμένη should come after πορευομένη. 'Walking in the fear of the Lord' would seem to be simply Christian Greek based on such O.T. passages as Ps. cxix. 1.

[1] De Zwaan appears not to note this case, but cf. Dodd, *Apostolic Preaching*, p. 37. On the other hand de Zwaan appears to accept an Aramaic original for the whole of the section ix. 31–xi. 18 on the very doubtful instances mentioned in the preceding note and the equally doubtful cases in the note following. It is quite possible that Peter's speech and the miracle stories come from an Aramaic original; but it need not be the same original. It must be remembered that form-criticism had hardly risen above the horizon when de Zwaan wrote in 1922.

it contains one or two rather dubious semitisms,[1] is written in Greek which shows very definite affinities with the second part of Acts, both in its methods of expression and in its use of typically Lucan words, and words which are classical though not found elsewhere in Luke. We may note than in x. 10 we find the word πρόσπεινος meaning 'hungry', which has hitherto been regarded as 'one of the dwindling number of N.T. words for which no parallel is known'. But is must be struck off the list, since the new Liddell and Scott gives one from a first century medical writer.[2] On the other hand this

---

[1] In x. 30 ἀπὸ τετάρτης ἡμέρας μέχρι ταύτης τῆς ὥρας is certainly awkward; but the explanation that μέχρι simply means 'about' or that it is due to a slip, either by Luke or an early copyist who was accustomed to the correlation ἀπό... μέχρι seems reasonable (*Beginnings of Christianity*, IV, 118). In x. 14 οὐδέποτε... πᾶν κοινόν is a semitism, but a Hebraism dependent on Ezek. iv. 14 (*ibid.* II, 50 and IV, 115). Torrey claims ἀρχαί of the corners of the sheet as an Aramaism, but the word in this sense has good Greek parallels–including Hippocrates.

[2] Of the prepositions, particles, etc. claimed by Clark as characteristic of Acts σύν makes three out of its twenty appearances in the first half of the book at x. 2, 20 and 23: τε makes three out of forty-seven at x. 22, 28 and 33, which would not be noticeable but for the fact that in each case it stands by itself, meaning 'and' and is not followed by καί; Moulton and Geden note twenty-six such uses in the first half of Acts, three of which are doubtful, but there seems no doubt in these three instances. Of other characteristic words ἀνήρ appears eleven times in the whole Cornelius incident, eight of these being between x. 1 and 30; it may be noted that it appears in the Lucan editorial insertion in ix. 38, while Aeneas is an ἄνθρωπος in ix. 33. συνέρχομαι appears three times between x. 1 and 30, once in the Lucan insertion at ix. 39 and once in the later part of the Cornelius story (xi. 12); we thus account for five out of nine appearances of the word in the first half of Acts. μηδείς makes two out of its eight appearances in these verses; it appears also in the continuation at xi. 12; φάναι makes three out of six.

Words only found in the Lucan writings in the N.T. include μεταπέμπεσθαι, μετακαλεῖσθαι, συνκαλεῖσθαι (in the Middle) and διαπορεῖν. Other words which are rarely found in the N.T. outside the Lucan

Lucan language is mainly confined to the opening part of the story and to those portions of it which are repeated in chap. xi. Moreover the narrative of x. 1–34 tells us nothing that is not to be found in xi. 4–15. I am inclined to suspect that we have before us the tradition of the founding of the Church (or the Gentile Church) at Caesarea in a narrative roughly of the length of xi. 4–15, which would be a story rather longer than the Marcan feeding of the 5,000 and shorter than the Gadarene swine. Such a narrative unit of tradition is easily intelligible; it might even have been combined in the Caesarean tradition with the originally independent miracle-stories which precede it in the present text of Acts. This story would seem to have been expanded with the story of the questioning of Peter's action on his return to Jerusalem and his defence; the repetition of the story gave it an added emphasis; whether it rests on anything more than the knowledge of the Church of Caesarea

writings or outside Luke and the better Greek writers of the N.T. include συναντᾶν (Luke 5, Heb. 2), πυνθάνεσθαι (Luke 9, Matt. 1, John 1), ἐξηγήσασθαι (Luke 5, John 1), ἀθέμιτος (Luke 1, 1 Pet. 1), ξενίζειν (= entertain: Luke 6, Heb. 1).

Words which are good Greek but not found elsewhere in the N.T. include μηδαμῶς (x. 14, repeated at xi. 8), ὁδοιπορεῖν, ἀναγκαῖος (of close personal friends, classical), ἀναντιρρητῶς (Polybius), διερωτᾶν. For διενθυμεῖσθαι L.S.J. give no parallel; ἀλλόφυλος (only here in the N.T.) is classical but may be taken by Luke from the LXX; this might apply to ἐξηγήσασθαι, found in the LXX seven times. ὅραμα in x. 17 (Luke 11, Matt. 1) is also from the LXX, which has supplied Peter's speech with εὐεργετεῖν and καταδυναστεύειν (once in James).

For πρόσπεινος as not found elsewhere cf. Voc.Gr.N.T., s.voc., followed by Beginnings of Christianity, IV, 115. L.S.J. quote Demosthenes Opthalmicus (First century A.D.) quoted by Aetius VII, 33, giving directions as to food to be given to patients ἐὰν πρόσπεινοι γένωνται. It is remarkable that Hobart misses this word.

It should be noted that Luke has not cut out the semitic ἰδού, frequent in the Gospel and Acts i–xii; for its use in the rest of Acts cf. above, p. 14.

that Peter's action had been questioned at Jerusalem and that
he had maintained his position successfully, we cannot say.
Luke found the story, and, to increase its importance to the
reader, decorated the original version of the whole incident
with some fine writing and chose it as a suitable place for one
of the various kerygmata of the Gospel which he had at his
disposal. He left the story of Cornelius very much in its
original form with a few consequential alterations to harmonise
the Caesarean narrative with his own stylistic improvements,
but transferred it to its present place as Peter's defence of himself at Jerusalem. The repetition may be intended to suit the
taste of his readers rather than to express his own approval of
the rather clumsy literary device.[1] Some such hypothesis seems
needed to explain the peculiarities of the whole incident as
recorded by Luke; in itself the story of Cornelius's conversion
is quite reasonable, once it is recognised that visions were
frequent in the atmosphere of primitive Christianity.[2]

[1] In view of the communal hatreds of Caesarea it is quite natural that
the first Gentile convert should be a soldier of Italian origin who would
have no particular sympathy with either side; as already an adherent of
the synagogue he would be acceptable to Jewish Christians. It must be
remembered that the Gentile Church of Caesarea would probably be
composed of people proud to call themselves Greeks, but with little or
no Greek blood in them, and with no Greek culture beyond a knowledge
of the koine and the LXX. They might easily regard this repetition as a
good way of emphasising the story of the foundation of a Gentile
community which had triumphed over Jewish opposition. Cf. above,
p. 28.

[2] For Peter's vision cf. Streeter, *Reality*, p. 329. Luke may have
added the detail that Cornelius's emissaries arrived immediately after
Peter's vision. On the other hand he does not make the visions of Peter
and Cornelius coincide, which we should expect on the normal methods
of hagiography (cf. Matt. xv. 28 as against Mark vii. 30, and John iv. 52 f.
and Matt. viii. 13 as against the version of the story in Luke vii. 10).
xi. 16 looks like a Lucan cross-reference to i. 4.

It has been suggested that Cornelius was never baptised on the

With xi. 19 we return to the tradition of the founding of the Church of Antioch, broken off at viii. 4; it gives in twelve verses the events of the same number of years; all it tells us is that the Hellenists at Antioch preached to the Gentiles, that the Church at Jerusalem sent Barnabas, apparently to insist that the Gentile converts must become proselytes of Judaism, and that Barnabas was so impressed by what he saw that instead of doing so, he called in Paul from Tarsus to help him.[1] The only incident recorded is the arrival of prophets from Jerusalem; they do not appear to have been interested in the question of the circumcision of Gentile converts; the statement that the famine foretold by them occurred in the reign of Claudius implies that the prophecy was uttered in the reign of some other emperor, who can only be Caligula. It is natural to suppose that the purpose of their visit was to support the Jewish protests against the proposal of Caligula to set up his statue in the Temple, a scheme which excited the horror of the Jewish Christians to an extent which can be judged from the marks which it has left in the N.T.[2] Luke carries on this story to its logical conclusion, the sending of alms to Jerusalem at the time of the famine, which appears to have reached its height in or about A.D. 47.[3] He then inserts from another source the story

---

strength of xi. 17 f., x. 47 being a Lucan insertion. But Luke is quite liable to omit the mention of baptism, cf. Acts xvii. 4, 34, xviii. 8, which might mean that Crispus was not baptised though 'many of the Corinthians' were. In fact he was baptised by Paul himself (1 Cor. i. 14).

[1] For this interpretation cf. *Jerusalem*, pp. 156 ff.

[2] Cf. *Jerusalem*, pp. 165 ff., and p. 187, n. 9.

[3] *G.J.V.* 1, 567. Torrey regards the statement that the famine extended 'over the whole world' as due to a misunderstanding of the Aramaic usage 'all the land', i.e. the whole of Judea, as meaning 'the whole earth'. De Zwaan (*Beginnings of Christianity*, 11, 59) well observes that a man who did not know the different meanings of the word ארעא did not know enough Aramaic to translate at all, and that the Lucan phrase is

of the Herodian persecution, Peter's escape and the death of Herod, and finally completes this part of his story by bringing Paul and Barnabas back from Jerusalem to Antioch for their first missionary journey.

Was this visit the same as the second visit to Jerusalem recorded in Gal. ii, the occasion of the agreement with the older Apostles and the circumcision of Titus? So far as the dates are concerned there is no reason to doubt it; Paul puts that visit fourteen years either after his conversion or after his first visit three years after his conversion. Assuming that his conversion took place in A.D. 35 and that the famine reached its height in A.D. 47, we get fourteen years, i.e. twelve years and bits of two others between the conversion and the crisis of the famine. We have no reason to suppose that Luke intends us to understand that Barnabas and Paul went up to Jerusalem immediately after the prophecy (they would have had precious little to bring unless they had collected week by week for a considerable period of time), and remained in the city throughout the whole reign of Herod with every hellenistic Jew thirsting for Paul's blood. Luke is merely following the normal practice of the ancient compiler of history in carrying on one source to a suitable stopping point before going on to another source.[1]

'a conscious heightening of colour, a common case of the "laws" of the growth of legendary narrative'. No doubt Agabus made the famine world-wide, for it was a sign of the imminence of the Second Coming foreshadowed by the appearance of the 'abomination of desolation' in the Temple; and after all there really was quite a bad famine.

[1] Better historians that Luke create difficulties for the reader in this way. Diodorus Siculus XVII, lxii, 1 introduces his account of the war of Agis by saying that in the archonship of Aristophon at Athens (beginning about midsummer 331 B.C.) and the consulship of C. Domitius and A. Cornelius at Rome (from Jan. 331) the news of the battle of Arbela led the cities of Greece to strike a blow for their freedom against Macedonia while the power of Persia still stood. This is nonsense; the power of

We shall have to deal with the whole question later; but to suppose that Luke can be charged with inaccuracy in his dating here is to show a complete ignorance of the methods of ancient historians.[1]

The events of chap. xii need not be drawn from a common source; it is of course possible that Peter's escape formed part of the collection of miracle-stories from which Aeneas and Tabitha are drawn, but if so it has been completely re-written. The wealth of detail is entirely beyond that of popular oral tradition: as an escape from prison it belongs to a class of miracle-story discussed below (p. 63). On the other hand Herod's death in the Lucan version is less miraculous than in that of Josephus; naturally it is regarded as a divine visitation by both writers. It would seem that all the incidents of this chapter, apart from the editorial last verse, are drawn

---

Persia fell at Arbela on 1 Oct. 331; the battle of Megalopolis occurred soon after (*C.A.H.* vi, 445). But Diodorus has already described Arbela under the events of the preceding year, in order to carry his source for Alexander's campaign up to its logical break, instead of stopping short with the archontic year of Athens. Tacitus, a far greater historian than Diodorus, has a similar difficulty. In *Ann.* XIII, 41 he describes Corbulo's campaign in Armenia, ending with the destruction of Artaxata at some unspecified date in A.D. 58. At XIV, 23 he returns to this part of his story with Corbulo's advance against Tigranocerta from the region of Artaxata in A.D. 59, having thus left Corbulo's army to face an Armenian winter in the ruins of Artaxata. Either he has carried the campaign of 58 up to the destruction of Artaxata in 59 in order to break off at a suitable point, or more probably he has antedated the destruction of the city from the spring of 59 to the autumn of 58 for the same reason (*C.A.H.* x, 762 and 880).

[1] For the text of xii. 25 (εἰς as against ἐξ) cf. *Beginnings of Christianity*, IV, 141. I cannot help feeling that ἐξ is right and that εἰς is due to a stupid copyist who was trying to harmonise Acts with Galatians and at the same time supposed that with ἐξ the text implies that Barnabas and Paul were in Jerusalem for the whole period covered by xii. 1–24.

from the oral tradition of the Church of Jerusalem,[1] though this raises a curious point. Luke's statement that Phoenicia depended on Palestine for its supply of grain is entirely true, and introduces a basic economic fact in the kind of parenthetical way which is found in the best historical writers. Of course both Luke and Josephus may be drawing on two different versions of the story, which may well have figured in some compilation of edifying tales of divine vengeance on men who allowed themselves to be regarded as gods (we can hardly imagine a Christian compilation of edifying stories of the death of persecutors as early as this). But it seems most unlikely that such a source would have troubled to record the economic fact, and it must be admitted that the detail suggests that Luke may have had a better eye for the basic fact of history than is usually allowed. Josephus does not mention the point; it could hardly be expected of him since he has no good source for this period.[2]

[1] Torrey claims θυμομαχῶν in verse 20 as an Aramaism, but it appears in Polybius (ix, xl, 4).

[2] For the facts cf. *G.J.V.* II, 77 with the references given there. For such incidental introductions of economic facts cf. Thucydides III, lxxxvi, 4, where we are given the real reason for the Athenian interest in Sicily in the quite casual reference to the fact that it served as a granary for the Peloponnese. In *Beginnings of Christianity*, IV, 139 it is suggested that 'a certain amount of historical setting irrelevant to the principal point of the event has remained in the narrative'. This seems to imply a written source, but gives no suggestion as to the nature of such a document. The most obvious kind of document would be a collection of edifying stories of divine punishments for ὕβρις ; Philo's *In Flaccum*, *Leg. ad Gaium* and his lost tract on Sejanus represent a monstrous writing up of stories with a moral, (here the divine vengeance on those who persecute the Jews). In this case we should be almost compelled to suppose that Luke is responsible for the detail. A good historian might of course have recorded the death of Herod as a punishment for ὕβρις and Luke might have carried over the irrelevant detail, but it is hard to conjecture who this historian can have been. It seems much more

To sum up the results of our discussion of sources I would suggest that apart from the speeches, representing a more or less fixed pattern of preaching, which may have been reduced to writing, we have in these chapters no written sources with the possible exception of chapters i to v inclusive, but excluding most of the speeches.[1] This source may have duplicated the trials before the Sanhedrin and included a miraculous escape from prison of dubious historical value; but it reached Luke with the doublets already in it. It remains possible that the whole section represents what Luke could collect by way of oral tradition for himself, and that the doublets are due to his failure to recognise that the two trials before the Sanhedrin really describe the same event. For the rest I can find no single unit which is likely in view of its length and the subject-matter to have been written down as a separate document; it seems far more probable that Luke has collected his material from oral tradition, often taking down his informant's words verbatim; it is just possible that he had a document describing the missionary journey of Peter which ended with the conversion of Cornelius.[2]

likely that Luke has drawn the whole story from what was public knowledge, as interpreted by the oral tradition of the Church of Jerusalem, and has inserted the detail from his own knowledge as a matter of interest in spite of its irrelevance.

For a similar story cf. the death of the tribune Aulus Pompeius as a punishment for insulting the Great Mother of Pessinus, Diod. Sic. xxxvi, xiii, 1 ff.

[1] Cf. above, p. 17. For Luke's failure to understand 'Peter's' testimony in ii. 33, cf. below, p. 84.

[2] The document, as we have seen, probably did not describe a journey, but simply some miracles of Peter and the foundation of the Gentile Church at Caesarea. But it is quite unnecessary to suppose that such a "document" existed.

CHAPTER III

GALATIANS AND THE COUNCIL OF JERUSALEM

At this point we must consider the central problem of Acts, a problem which affects not only the question of sources but also the whole credibility of Luke as a historian. If the Council of Jerusalem, as described in Acts xv, is Luke's version of the meeting of Paul with the 'pillars' in Gal. ii. 1–14, it is usually held that the discrepancy between the two accounts is so wide that Luke's credit as a historian is gone. Acts must be the work, not of the companion of Paul who writes in the first person, but of an ignorant compiler, who knew little of Paul and had never read his Epistles. We cannot rely on anything in Acts unless it can be corroborated by the Pauline letters, or unless it appears in the we-sections, which may still represent the travel-diary of a companion of Paul which somehow came into the hands of the compiler.

It must be observed in the first place that there are considerable difficulties about this compiler. It has been noticed above (pp. 1 f.) that Acts is one of the books of the N.T. which have contributed to the Greek of Ignatius. Further, Ignatius knows the Pastoral Epistles, notably 2 Tim. (*Trall.* vii. 2 = 2 Tim. i. 3; the 'wolves' which 'capture' the Christian in *Philad.* ii. 2 present a mixed metaphor which originates in the combination of John x. 12 or Acts xx. 29 with 2 Tim. iii. 6; *Smyrn.* i. 1 σοφίσαι is from 2 Tim. iii. 15; (the verb in the active meaning 'to make wise' is found in the LXX Psalter (xix. 8, cxix. 98), but Ignatius has the smallest possible acquaintance with the O.T., and probably only through Christian sources; *L.S.J.* give no other parallels); *ibid.* ix. 1 = 2 Tim. ii. 25 f.;

ibid. x. 2 Tim. i. 16; *Polyc.* vi, 2 Tim. ii. 4).[1] Now the writer of 2 Tim. appears to have drawn his knowledge of Paul's career in iii. 11 from Acts; he knew that Timothy came from Derbe and that there had been more or less successful attacks on Paul at Antioch, Iconium and Lystra, though he omitted to notice Philippi (Acts xiii. 50, xiv. 5 and 19; apart from Philippi these are the only places in Paul's journeys as recorded in Acts where he does not escape from or triumph over his persecutors). Thus we have to imagine a compiler who is interested enough in Paul to write his life, yet does not know his Epistles, since he has never read Galatians. Yet he is early enough for his works to be accepted by the author of 2 Tim., which again is early enough for Ignatius to be familiar with it and to treat it as scripture, while Ignatius was martyred before A.D. 117. Yet again he is not early enough to have access to any authentic account of Paul's travels or Paul's theology. It cannot be said that it is impossible to find a date for our compiler, but he involves a fairly heavy strain on the imagination.

It may further be observed that Luke's credit as a writer need not depend so completely on a reconciliation of Acts xv and Gal. ii as is sometimes supposed. If we assume that the account of the Council existed as an independent document possessed by one of the great Churches and representing the events of Gal. ii in this way, it is quite possible that Luke, if he came across it, might have inserted it bodily in his narrative. He might indeed have been moved to put it at this point by the fact that he was intelligent enough to see that it could not be regarded as a duplicate of the story of Gal. ii in view of the

---

[1] Ignatius's Greek is largely made up of these reminiscences of the N.T.; the rest comes from pagan religion and astrology. The force of the argument above lies largely in the fact that a large part of his letters are a cento of N.T. words and phrases; a close investigation of his vocabulary is badly needed.

obvious inconsistencies of the two stories; consequently he inserted it at what he regarded as an appropriate point.

On the other hand it must be asked whether we are compelled to identify the Council of Acts xv with the visit of Gal. ii. Lightfoot attempted to accept the identification and at the same time to save Luke's credit by arguments which are quite unconvincing, as for instance that Paul did indeed go up to Jerusalem for the famine-visit; but owing to the Herodian persecution none of the Apostles were in Jerusalem, so that he only saw the presbyters and felt at liberty to ignore that visit. This would be a quite puerile bit of mendacity. Paul is concerned to prove his independence of those 'who were in Christ before him'; and among the presbyters there must have been many who had seen Jesus in His earthly life and could have told him much of what the Lord had done and taught. Equally unconvincing is his suggestion that the concordat with James and 'Cephas' is Paul's version of the Council and describes a private agreement made by Paul with the 'pillars' of the Church which was subsequently ratified by a full meeting of the members of the Church of Jerusalem; we have no reason for supposing that the Church had by this date reached that stage of democracy in which the public meeting registers its assent to a decision reached in advance by its leading members. Lightfoot's argument (*Galatians*, pp. 123 ff.) that the geography is the same has no real force, since any controversies on this subject at this period were bound to centre round Jerusalem and Antioch; the persons involved are not the same, John being absent in Acts; the result is not the same, since in Galatians Paul and Barnabas are given a vague recognition as Apostles of the Gentiles with a free hand in the matter of the observance of the Law, but there is nothing to prevent Peter from refusing to eat with the Gentiles. Lightfoot's argument from the similarity of the Roman and Galatian epistles that they must have been written at about the same date is quite unconvincing. The resemblances are indeed close and numerous, but he does not notice how largely they are dictated by the subject of the letters and the traditional Jewish method of arguing from the O.T. Thus Paul's favourite proof-text 'Abraham believed in God and it was counted to him for righteousness' is also a favourite proof-text of Philo, though Philo does not use it to support a doctrine of justification by faith.[1] On the other hand the purpose of the letters is entirely different; Galatians is a flaming attack on Jewish Christians who are perverting the Gospel; Romans is Paul's elaborate apologia as against his own nation. The difference is reflected in the barbarous style of Galatians, as for instance in the hopeless anacoluthon of ii. 3 f. and the transition from the answer to Peter to Paul's own theology at ii. 14 ff. Nor in Romans have we the satirical excursion into rabbinical methods which we find in Gal. iii.[2] On the other hand Galatians has nothing like the elaborately artificial parody of the rhetoric of the synagogues of the Dispersion in Romans i. 18 ff., or the skilful writing and the excursion into hellenistic Jewish philosophy in ii. 1 ff.[3] In fact if we were to apply Clark's linguistic tests to the two Epistles, we should

[1] Cf. *Hellenistic Elements*, p. 35.

[2] For the arguments of Gal. iii. 13 and 20 cf. *Gentiles*, p. 108. For the argument from 'seeds' and 'seed' in 16, which looks at first sight like a grossly disingenuous piece of special pleading, cf. Mishnah *Shabb.* ix. 2 (tr. Danby). Here it is argued that if a garden-bed be six handbreadths square, it becomes not a bed but a garden, in which six varieties of seed may be sown without transgressing the law as to *Kilaim*; this is proved by Is. lxi. 11, which says 'As the garden causes the seeds which are sown in it to spring forth'. It is written not "its seed", but "the seeds which are sown in it".' Paul is writing to warn his opponents that if it comes to rabbinical methods of argument he is a better rabbi than any of them. We have nothing of this sort in Romans.

[3] Cf. *Hellenistic Elements*, pp. 31 ff.

43

be obliged to throw the whole tradition of N.T. criticism into the most disastrous confusion by holding that Romans and Galatians cannot be by the same writer (cf. above, p. 10). Of course this does not prove that they were not written at approximately the same time; it only proves that Paul was fighting for his life and in an extremely bad temper when he wrote Galatians, but had recovered when he wrote Romans. But if he could use the same arguments in two such different frames of mind, he could also use them after an interval of several years when writing on a similar subject though with an entirely different purpose.

Thus there is nothing in the internal evidence of Galatians and Romans to compel us to identify the Council of Acts xv with the conference of Gal. ii. Nor can Luke be accused of suppressing the truth in not mentioning the conference and the affair of Titus, if they happened during the famine-visit. He records the beginnings of the discussion with the conversion of Cornelius and the end with the Council; intermediate stages could be omitted when they led to no decisive result and aroused painful memories. In this particular case there were good reasons why the Jewish Christians should not accept the decision of the 'pillars' of the Church recorded in Gal. ii, if that decision was reached during the famine-visit. In the first place that decision had failed to produce a final settlement in view of Peter's failure to stand by it (or by Paul's interpretation of it) at Antioch. In the second place that decision had been reached at a time when the Pauline missions were confined to a fairly small area in Syria and Cilicia. It might reasonably be hoped that their proximity to Palestine would lead them to see the wisdom of accepting the Torah as a safeguard against the danger of relapsing into the vices of the Gentiles; in any case that proximity and the influence of the Jewish Church and Jewish converts in these Churches would do much to counteract the danger. It was quite another matter if Paul was to travel up and down the world converting all and sundry; there would be far more Gentiles than the Church could hope to absorb without a grave danger to her whole standard of morality. This was a danger in the face of which Judaisers might well renew their perfectly sincere attempt to preserve the Church from what they reasonably regarded as an appalling menace.[1]

With regard to the arguments brought against the historicity of the Council on the ground of the speeches, they are entirely beside the mark; Luke's speeches are not historical in the sense that they are summaries of what was said. Torrey's attempt to find Aramaisms in them are quite unconvincing;[2] it is hard to imagine that an Aramaic original would represent James as quoting Amos i x. 11 f. from the LXX to make a point which the Hebrew version could not prove. It is urged that Peter could not use the very language of Paulinism as he does in xv. 9 f.; this may or may not be true, but certainly Luke would feel perfectly justified in representing him as doing so, if he knew that Peter had later, if not at so early a stage, accepted the general Pauline view. Similarly he would have felt quite justified in putting into James's mouth a favourite testimony from the LXX to prove God's intention of converting the Gentiles; he probably would not have known that there was any difference between the Greek and Hebrew at this point; he would certainly have held that the Greek was right as against the Hebrew, since it foretold that purpose of con-

---

[1] It is unfortunate that the anti-Jewish prejudices of many continental scholars makes them fail to realise the strength of the judaising position. No doubt the sins of the Gentiles were often exaggerated by the Jews, as they are in Paul's parody of synagogue rhetoric in Romans i. 24 ff. But the reality of the danger is proved by 1 Corinthians.

[2] Cf. de Zwaan in *Beginnings of Christianity*, II, 48 f.

45

verting the Gentiles which was already being fulfilled; obviously a version which contained a true prophecy must be the right one. He certainly would not have credited James with the power to distinguish the true from the false version. The argument that Peter who in the affair of Cornelius prided himself on never having eaten anything common or unclean could not here refer to the Torah as a yoke, which neither we nor our fathers were able to bear, misses the whole point of the Council. It is not dealing simply with the demand of the Judaisers that Gentile converts must be circumcised, but with the demand of the Pharisees that they must be circumcised and commanded to keep the law of Moses. In their mouth as in Paul's, (Gal. v. 3 and vi. 13) 'the Law' meant the whole law as interpreted by the Pharisees; the popular standard of observance on which Peter prided himself was no better than living like a Gentile.[1] To Peter and the ordinary Jew of Galilee, and probably of Judaea, this was an attempt to impose an intolerable burden.

Equally unconvincing is the argument that Paul could not

[1] Cf. *Jerusalem*, pp. 224 ff. In spite of the evidence of the New Testament and the tract *Demai* in the Mishnah it is commonly assumed by Jewish scholars that the ordinary Jew of the period lived by the rules of the Mishnah. The only evidence for this is Jos. *Antt.* XVIII, 15 which merely states that their doctrine of immortality makes the Pharisees popular, and that questions as to vows and sacrifices are regulated by their decisions. Josephus is never above suspicion unless we know his source; here he may be correct, since the Mishnah supports him as to sacrifices (*Yoma* i, 3, 5); his statement as to their leniency in punishment is not borne out by such passages as *Makkoth* i, 5. Josephus himself includes a violently anti-pharisaical passage (? from Nicolas of Damascus) in *Antt.* XIII, 409 ff., (= *B.J.* I, 110 ff.) an illuminating comment on his reliability. Both the Gospels and Acts show that there was little love lost between them and the ordinary Galilean Jew. For Gal. v. 3 cf. *Judaism*, I. 331, quoting R. Judah the Patriarch.

have agreed to the food-laws laid down by the Council.[1] If he had gained his main point, that the Gentile converts need not be circumcised, there was no reason why he should not accept a rule with regard to food which was harmless in itself, and was at the moment rightly regarded as essential to the common life of the Church. It was circumcision that was the obstacle to any widespread conversion of the Gentiles in view of the Greek dislike of mutilation of any kind.[2] On the other hand sharing in the common meal and eucharist was the centre of the life of the Church. If Jews would not eat with uncircumcised Gentiles at Antioch, it meant that Gentiles would become an inferior caste in the Church; but with the growth of Gentile Churches a refusal to recognise the Jewish law as to *kosher* meat would mean that the Jews would be in danger of becoming an inferior caste; and this would be equally undesirable.[3] It is true that

[1] The reading of D here is the clearest proof of the secondary character of the peculiar variations of its text. The decrees of the Council lapsed in a very short time, since they were intended for mixed communities of Jews who still observed the Law and Gentiles who did not. If such Churches were to share a common meal, Jewish rules must be observed. But outside Palestine the Jewish members of a mainly Gentile Church would normally cease to observe the Jewish law in view of the very grudging toleration of their views by the Church. Justin *Dial.* 47 (265 D) holds that they will be saved if they do not try to impose their views on others, but admits that he is a liberal in the matter. The Bezan reading is an attempt to accommodate the decision of the Council to the state of affairs in the Church known to the reviser; but an alteration of the text in the opposite sense is quite unthinkable.

[2] Cf. *Gentiles*, p. 62; Nock, *St Paul*, p. 104.

[3] For the difficulties of the grammar and text of xv. 28 cf. *Beginnings of Christianity*, IV, 180, and *Voc.Gr.N.T.*, *s.voc.*, from which it would seem that the objection of the former that there 'is little if any evidence for ἐπάναγκες as an...impersonal verb' cannot be sustained in view of P. Ryl. II, 65, 5 (? 67 B.C.) and Menander, Fr. p. 176. In view of this the suggestion that τῶν is simply due to dittography from τούτων is attractive.

his acceptance of such a regulation is inconsistent with his teaching in Galatians and Romans, that the whole conception of law as such has ceased to apply to the Christian. But he is perfectly willing to lay down a new system of law for the Church in 1 Corinthians in order to prevent Christians from going to law before Gentile judges or to force women to wear hats in Church. Paul's failure to allude to the decrees in 1 Cor. viii. 1 ff.[1] is easily intelligible in view of the situation at Corinth; it would have been futile to appeal to the Council against the disorderly elements which claimed a complete liberty 'in Christ'; it would only have strengthened the case of the Jewish opponents who refused to recognise him as an Apostle in the full sense if he had appealed to any authority but his own, without producing any impression on the Gentiles. For the Gentile converts (perhaps already a majority at Corinth) would at this period have no reason for regarding themselves as members of a world-wide Church, an idea only intelligible to those familiar with the conception of Judaism as the religion of a nation spread throughout the world.[2] Paul's antinomian opponents would simply have answered that such decisions might bind the ordinary Christian, but could not affect those who had the higher gnosis which enabled them to realise that, since idols were nothing, there could be no harm in eating

[1] For the objection on these grounds cf. Windisch in *Beginnings of Christianity*, II, 326.

[2] For the view put forward above cf. *Jerusalem*, p. 326, n. 31. For the absence of the idea of solidarity among the votaries of the various pagan cults in different cities cf. Nock, *Conversion*, pp. 135 and 241; in the latter passage he seems to underestimate the solidarity of Judaism. Each synagogue was independent, but they looked to a common centre at Jerusalem and visits to the Holy City seem to have been fairly frequent, while any Jew of eminence would claim the respect of any synagogue he visited and would also regard it as his duty to criticise its short-comings.

sacrificial meats. On the other hand, too strict an insistence on abstaining from meats offered to idols would make life impossible for Gentile converts who could not deal with Jewish butchers; and it is clear from Romans xi. 13 ff. that the Gentile converts were already beginning to regard themselves as superior to Jewish Christians. In consequence Paul is concerned to establish a Christian moral code on the basis of reason; it is hard to see what other course he could have adopted with any prospect of success.

As against these objections it must be observed that on the assumption that Galatians was written before the Council, we get a perfectly clear historical development. Peter is compelled by the affair of Cornelius to recognise the possibility of the baptism of uncircumcised Gentiles, and during the famine-visit he with James and John agree to leave Paul a free-hand in preaching to the Gentiles. At Antioch he wavers under Jewish pressure to the extent of refusing to eat with them. Paul protests indignantly, but without success. The result is the decision of the Church of Antioch to launch a vigorous Gentile mission. This brings matters to a head: some Jewish converts demand the circumcision of all converts, with an amount of success in Paul's newly-founded 'Galatian' Churches which provokes the epistle to the Galatians. The whole question is referred to a council at Jerusalem, but the demand of the Judaisers is neutralised by the claims of the Christian Pharisees that circumcision by itself is worthless. Gentiles, no less than Jews, are bound 'to keep the law of Moses' in the sense of the Pharisees. This is opposed by Peter, who represents the ordinary standard of Judaism at the Council. James, the leading Pharisee, proposes a compromise which abandons the Torah, so far as Gentile converts are concerned, and is content to issue a warning against the sins conventionally ascribed to the Gentiles by

Jewish writers, and to insist on rules as to the killing of animals for meat which will make it possible for Jewish converts to attend the common meals of the Church. The speech is no doubt a free composition by Luke which he regards as being in keeping with the character of the speaker. The result is the acceptance of James's proposal, which is embodied in a circular to the Gentile Churches, the peculiarities of which suggest that we are dealing with an original document copied by Luke more or less verbatim; it is hard to see why he should have introduced the curious phrase οἱ πρεσβύτεροι ἀδελφοί unless he found it in his original, or to suppose that in writing an imaginary letter some years later he would have been bold enough to represent the Church of Jerusalem as writing 'it seemed good to the Holy Ghost and to us'.[1] Even the curious fact that the letter is ostensibly addressed to 'the brethren in Syria and Cilicia' supports its authenticity. The Churches founded on the recent Pauline journey might at the time be regarded as a relatively small extension of the existing Churches at the Syrian Antioch and Tarsus rather than as the beginning of a

---

[1] For the πρεσβύτεροι ἀδελφοί cf. the πρεσβύτεροι ἱερεῖς of some Egyptian Temples quoted in *Voc.Gr.N.T.*, *s.voc.* There seems no reason why Luke should use the curious phrase as against πρεσβύτεροι in xiv. 23, xv. 4, 6, etc., unless he found it in the original, or unless he knew at least that it was a characteristic phrase of the early Church at Jerusalem. A late compiler is out of the question. 'It seemed good to the Holy Ghost and to us' is no less difficult. The nearest approach to such a bold expression is 1 Cor. v. 3; 1 Cor. vii. 10 and 1 Thess. iv. 15 would be comparable if they mean that Paul claims to be speaking with full divine authority; but it seems more likely that Paul claims, rightly or wrongly, to be quoting words which go back to Jesus Himself. Individual prophets and πνευματικοί might claim to speak in the Spirit with divine authority, but there is no parallel for such a phrase to pronounce a corporate decision by a deliberative body. For the letter cf. Meyer, *Urspr. u. Anf.* III, 187 ff.

new appeal to the Gentile world.[1] The result of the letter is a final settlement of the controversy; Paul later writes in Romans a reasoned defence of his position as against his own people, and though we read from time to time of Jewish Christians who question his apostolic authority, there is no organised attempt to impose circumcision and the keeping of the Mosaic law on Gentile converts. It is indeed possible that these Jewish Christians, if they could have got rid of Paul, would have gone on to urge the imposition of the Law, but in fact they did not succeed.[2]

It must be admitted that at one point Luke has been guilty of an inaccuracy. In xv. 36 he represents Paul as proposing to Barnabas a second visit to the Churches of Galatia as if it were a new idea, while in xvi. 4 the decrees of the Council are given to the new Churches. Clearly it was a matter of urgent necessity to inform them of the decision of the Council as soon as possible.

---

[1] The words might seem to be a strong argument in favour of the view that the letter was sent out at the time of the famine-visit, on the assumption that the conference of Gal. ii. took place then. But this would imply that the letter is an exact copy of a letter sent on that occasion which Paul has not mentioned; and it is very difficult to suppose that Paul would not have mentioned it. Luke or a later compiler would have mentioned the Churches of the second journey; the Church of Jerusalem at the time may well have regarded them as simply an extension of Paul's missions in Cilicia.

The Greek of the letter is good, but there is no reason to suppose that the Church of Jerusalem could not command the services of a good Greek letter-writer.

[2] Cf. 1 Cor. ix. 1 ff., 2 Cor. i. 15 ff., iii. 1 ff., xi. 1 ff. In these Epistles there is only one mention of circumcision (1 Cor. vii. 19) and here it is mentioned as something irrelevant. In Phil. it reappears (iii. 2), but again in reference to controversies with Jews, not Jewish Christians. It is of course possible that the Jewish Christian opponents would have tried to revive the whole matter if they could have succeeded in discrediting Paul's authority; but there is no evidence that they actually did so.

Luke has certainly been guilty of a very slovenly bit of writing. But the importance of the section xv. 36 ff. is the story of the quarrel between Paul and Barnabas. It is quite probable that there was in fact a considerable delay between the decision of the Council and the new journey, since the later stages of the first journey and the subsequent discussions ending in the Council may well have occupied a whole summer. The decision could have been conveyed to the Churches of Syria and Cilicia at once; but the passage of the Taurus range in winter was a difficult and dangerous matter.[1] Moreover it is possible that the inconsistency between xv. 36 and xvi. 4 is due to a change of source; at xvi. 1 ἰδού indicates that we are dealing with Paul's reminiscences; its absence at xvi. 9 suggests that we have already begun the we-section of xvi. 10 ff.[2] Naturally the 'source' in one case need be no more than Paul's verbal account of his quarrel with Barnabas and the circumcision of Timothy, in the other Luke's own free compilation, which may or may not have existed in a written form, before he compiled Acts;

---

[1] Cf. Ramsay in Hastings *DB*. extra volume, p. 377.

[2] Windisch objects (*Beginnings of Christianity*, II, 320) to the story of the circumcision of Timothy. 'According to 2 Tim. i. 5 Timothy had a pious Jewish mother and grandmother. It is hard to believe that Paul would have undertaken what these two women did not feel necessary and that out of respect for the Jews.' But there is no reason to suppose that the author of 2 Tim. has any evidence apart from the Acts and his own imagination; it is most unlikely that the pious mother and grandmother have any basis in history; the mixed marriage suggests a considerable laxity. (Cf. *Beginnings of Christianity*, IV, 184.) In any case the Gentile father would decide as to the son's circumcision, though in Jewish law the son of a Jewess must be circumcised. As an adult Timothy could of course decide for himself; Paul's action was strictly in accordance with his principles (1 Cor. ix. 19 ff.). It may be regrettable that Paul did not hold strongly anti-semitic views; but in fact he did not.

For ἰδού cf. p. 14; p. 32, n. 1.

we find similar inconsistencies in writers who are far more pretentious historians than Luke.[1]

[1] Thus in *Antt.* XIV, 131 Josephus describes how Antipater and Mithridates of Pergamum came to help Caesar in Egypt in the autumn of 48 B.C. (For the history cf. *C.A.H.* IX, 671 ff.) After they had taken Pelusium the Jews who held the 'district of Onias' opposed their advance, until Antipater showed them letters from Hyrcanus urging them in his capacity as High Priest to assist Caesar. At 138 however he writes that 'it is said by many that Hyrcanus took part in this expedition and came to Egypt' and quotes Asinius Pollio and Hypsicrates as being quoted to this effect by Strabo without regard to the fact that the narrative of the source which he is following at 131 makes the presence of Hyrcanus out of the question. But he cannot resist the opportunity of introducing one of the few favourable mentions of the Jews by a pagan writer which were available. Cf. *F.G.H.* 91, F. 16 and notes.

CHAPTER IV

THE ACTS AND HISTORY

In the second half of Acts, if the foregoing arguments are accepted, we are no longer concerned with Luke's sources. The evidence of style and language, even the slipshod methods of revision, all point to the same hand as responsible for compiling the story of Paul's journeys and the writing of the travel-story in which the writer records his presence by the use of 'we'.[1] It has indeed been urged that, even if we take the view that the Council in Acts xv and the dispute of Gal. ii are not the same event, Acts is guilty of a serious suppression of the truth, since it has no mention of the dispute at the time of the famine-visit[2] and no mention of the dispute between Peter and Paul at Antioch. The actual problems of this much-debated section of Acts we have already considered. But, on the assumption that we are really dealing with two separate incidents, it shows a complete ignorance of the ancient methods of writing history (and Luke would probably have been much surprised to find himself treated as a historian) to suppose that Luke's credibility is seriously compromised by his failure to record

[1] There is no evidence as to whether Luke was in Paul's company during the whole of his imprisonment at Caesarea or not. He could not accompany Paul during his hurried journey under escort from Jerusalem to Caesarea (xxiii. 31); he would hardly feel it necessary to insert the detail that 'hearing that Paul had been sent to Caesarea, we followed him thither'. In general his failure to mention the circumstances in which he joined or left Paul is strictly parallel to that of Ammianus Marcellinus, who does indeed mention how he came to be on the staff of Ursicinus ('cui nos obsecuturos iunxerat imperiale praeceptum,' XIV, ix, 1), but afterwards flits in and out as 'we' (XIV, xi, 5; XVI, x, 21; XVIII, vi, 5) or 'I' (XVIII, vi, 11) with no sort of explanation.

[2] Cf. Windisch in *Beginnings of Christianity*, II, 322.

the settlement at Jerusalem and its breakdown when Peter visited Antioch. To the ancient historian history was the course of events as determined by great personalities;[1] the actions of the less considerable mass of mankind were a side-issue, which could be ignored except in so far as it affected the great personalities. Further it was quite reasonable to sum up the whole of a long series of events by recording the decisive incident which settled it. But Luke was neither a historian nor, in the strict sense of the word a biographer. His theme was the advance of Christianity from Jerusalem to Rome as a result of the work of his hero, Paul, and the form which imposed itself on him was that of the travel story. Such stories, whether true or fictitious, appealed to the popular taste by providing a variety of scenes and adventures with plenty of marvels thrown in. The travelling philosopher was a well-known phenomenon and Paul's missions could be described in this light in a form which was true as far as it went, while at the same time it contained an element of miracle and adventure to suit the popular taste, combined with valuable propaganda on behalf of Christianity in an interesting and readable form.[2] Mark had already

---

[1] Cf. Meyer, *Gesch. des Alterthums*, III, 270 ff. on Thucydides. It is of course ludicrous to compare Luke with Thucydides as a historian, but his critics often expect of him a standard of accuracy which Thucydides himself could hardly live up to.

[2] Cf. Norden, *Agnostos Theos*, pp. 34 ff., for this type of literature as the model for the second part of Acts (which he wrongly regards as the work of another than the final compiler). For the fictitious literature of this type cf. Rohde, *Der Griechische Roman*[2], 183 ff., and the satire on such literature in Lucian's *Ver. Hist.* I, 3 (ed. Jacobitz, II, 71 ff.); we have an actual specimen in a summary form in his *De Mort. Peregr.* 9 ff. (ed. Jacobitz, III, 331 ff.). For the actual travels of Dio Chrysostom cf. v. Arnim, *Dio v. Prusa*, pp. 152 ff. Philostratus' life of Apollonius of Tyana is of course the best-known specimen of this class of literature, but Origen, *c. Cels.* VI, 41, refers to a life by Moiragenes. Lucian's allusions imply a large class of popular literature of this kind.

led the way by combining all the information he possessed about Jesus into such a form; it was the easier for him to do so since his materials seem to have included genuine traditions of the journeys in which He 'went about doing good'.[1] Luke had already thrown the materials for his Gospel which he did not draw from Mark or Q into the form of an account of the last journey of Jesus from Galilee to Jerusalem.[2] So much was he influenced by this literary type that in the first half of Acts, after the introductory chapters describing the establishment of the Church in Jerusalem, he throws the whole of his material into the form of travel-stories, two resulting from the death of Stephen, while the third is a journey of Peter compiled out of traditions which were already localised, so that Luke had only to connect them in order to make them into a travel-story.

It is only within the limits of what he set out to do that Luke can fairly be criticised. There is much that we should like to know which we are not told, for example as to the methods of government of the Pauline Churches, their forms of worship, the general social and economic status of the converts, the proportion of Jews and proselytes to Gentile converts, the minor controversies and the methods of settling them, and the beginnings of heretical movements among them. They did not fall within Luke's scheme and therefore he does not record them; they would not have interested his readers, who knew

[1] It is usual to suppose that the journeys are a purely Marcan 'framework'. But the repetition of the journey with a warning of the Passion in ix. 30 ff., and x. 32 ff. is only explicable if Mark had a fragment to this effect in two sources, both of which he included. It is not of course to be doubted that Jesus in fact worked largely through an itinerant ministry. But the casting of a book intended for religious purposes into the form of a travel-story seems to have been due to the desire to interest the reader; in Mark's case the use of the form may have been due to instinct rather than to deliberate imitation.

[2] Cf. Creed, *op. cit.* p. 140.

all about such details, and while they would have been intensely interesting to the modern critic it may be doubted whether they would interest the majority of modern Christian readers of his work. Other ancient writers tell us little on these matters; the summaries of the story of the early Church in Acts ii. 43 ff., iv. 4 and 32 ff. are very rare of their kind and they are intended not to be a historical record but to edify the reader. In general these are the matters on which ancient historians give us little information; we have only to consider how little we should know of the religious life of contemporary Judaism if Josephus were our only authority to see that Luke compares favourably with him in regard to the amount he tells us.[1]

As against this the interest of the reader is kept alive by a continual change of scene; each city is evangelised, there is normally a breach with the Jews and an account of the reasons for Paul's departure. Apart from this framework we have an incident or group of incidents (the breach with the Jews may itself be the main incident as at Thessalonica), illustrating Paul's methods of preaching or recording some miracles or the difficulties and opposition which he had to face. In some cases the intervening stages of his journey are described with minute accuracy, even when there is nothing to relate (xiii. 4 f., 13 f., xvii. 1 and 14 ff.); naturally this reaches its maximum in the we-sections. But where Paul is travelling over old ground, except in the we-sections, there may be only a bare summary; thus in the section xviii. 18–23 and xix. 1 Paul is taken from Corinth to Ephesus, where he conducts a preliminary mission to the synagogue, and thence to Caesarea, Jerusalem, Antioch, the 'Phrygian and Galatian country' and so back to Ephesus

[1] It is interesting to note how much of our information on pagan religion in so far as it is drawn from literary sources comes from the *Metamorphoses* of Apuleius, a 'novel with a purpose' in the form of a travel-story, apparently based on an entirely unedifying romance of the travel type.

in six verses. On the other hand a large part of the same itinerary is described at length in xx. 5 f., 13–16 and xxi. 1–3, 7 and 15 with various incidents inserted; the reason would seem to be that the writer incorporated his notes of the journey as they stood, but they have in fact a freshness which makes them very good reading and a Greek public had a fondness for such descriptions which would make them even more welcome to Luke's original readers than to us.

With Paul's imprisonment at Jerusalem this method has to be abandoned; yet even so the journey from Jerusalem to Caesarea is a really exciting piece of narrative, while in general the appearance of figures of high rank in the Roman and Jewish world keep the interest alive until we come to the climax of the whole, the story of the shipwreck.[1] At Rome Paul has to address the leading Jews of the city as if they knew nothing of Christianity beyond the vaguest rumours, although we have already heard that Paul had been met outside the city by representatives of the Church.[2] Moreover after a whole day spent in discussion Paul rejects the Jews of Rome as a whole with the testimony of Is.vi. 9 f.,[3] in spite of the fact that we have just

[1] Cf. *Hellenistic Elements*, p. 13. It may be noted that Luke has omitted what must have been a more thrilling shipwreck, alluded to in 2 Cor. xi. 25. The reason is that he does not profess to give a complete account of Paul's travels; but the shipwreck on the last voyage to Rome keeps the suspense of the reader at its highest pitch until the very last.

[2] Naturally the modern critic is disappointed when Luke misses his chance of telling us how far Christianity had really affected the Jewish colony at Rome at the time of Paul's arrival, and what the effect of Paul's Epistle had been. But Luke would see no point in mentioning what many of his readers knew already, while the rest could easily find out if they were curious.

[3] Luke minimises this in its Marcan position (Mark iv. 12 = Luke viii. 10), where it would seem to imply that the Jews had been condemned in advance by the foreknowledge of God. Luke at least gives them every possible chance before the final rejection at Rome.

been told that some of them believed. Now there is no reason to doubt that Paul held such a conference, or that the conference lasted from morning to evening, or that some of the Jews were convinced, while others were not. It is quite reasonable to suppose that Paul sent the unbelievers away with the prophecy of Isaiah, though it is by no means certain. For Luke is concerned here to dramatise Paul's arrival in Rome as the last chance of repentance offered to the Jewish nation as a whole; henceforth Paul's dealings with his own nation are at an end; the sequel was to describe Paul's dealings with Caesar.[1]

This is the general theme of Acts and the class of literature to which it belongs, and if we recognise it we immediately see that a large number of the so-called historical difficulties of Acts disappear. It says much for Luke's veracity that he has preserved Silas and Timothy as Paul's companions, although they are mere lay-figures. On the other hand we see how ridiculous is the fuss that has been made about the movements of these companions. In Acts xvii. 14 f. Paul leaves them at Beroea and goes on to Athens; here he waits for them, but before they come he goes on to Corinth, where they join him (xviii. 5). But it appears from 1 Thess. iii. 1 that Paul or, more probably, Paul and Silas, were content to be left alone at Athens, while

---

[1] The ending of Acts is no more a real ending than that of the Gospel; both presuppose a sequel. It is possible that Luke published them as he wrote them and broke off Acts because Paul's two years' imprisonment made a natural pause in the narrative. There may however have been some other landmark in his story (Peter's arrival in Rome or Paul's trial before Caesar) which made a suitable opening for his third part, in which the destruction of Jerusalem fulfilled the prophecies of the rejection of the Jews; the Neronian persecution, the martyrdom of Peter and Paul and possibly God's vengeance on Nero, furnished plenty of material for a book which could end with the imminent expectation of the Parousia. It is of course quite possible that the third part was never begun, but it seems unthinkable that it was not intended.

Timothy was sent on a mission to Thessalonica.[1] If so, it would seem that Timothy and Silas joined Paul at Athens, and that one or both of them were sent back to Thessalonica or Philippi and finally rejoined Paul at Corinth. It has been urged that we have here an inaccuracy which proves that we cannot have in Acts the work of a close companion of Paul. It proves nothing of the kind; the only reason for mentioning that they were left at Beroea in the first instance seems to be to show that Paul did not really intend to preach either at Athens or at Corinth but to return to Palestine. But he was provoked to preach by the idolatry of Athens and constrained by the Spirit to preach at Corinth instead of returning.[2]

Here we are dealing only with minor movements of minor characters. It has however been urged that in describing Paul's stay at Ephesus Luke has suppressed vital facts in order to avoid unedifying stories of controversies, or because Acts is the work of an ignorant compiler.[3] But from Luke's point of view the controversies at Corinth were quite unimportant. If 2 Cor. i–ix represents Paul's last word in the matter, the remaining chapters being part of Paul's earlier angry letter, the disputes at Corinth had been brought to a satisfactory conclusion before Paul left Ephesus; the unsuccessful visit to Corinth described in 2 Cor. ii. 1 did not fall within his scheme any more than Paul's journey to Arabia, or his ministry, extending over a large part of fourteen years in Tarsus and Cilicia, or the visit which he presumably paid to Jerusalem to secure Silas' help for his second journey,[4] or the visits to outlying parts of the province

---

[1] In view of 1 Thess. ii. 18 it is hard to take the 'we' of iii. 1 as purely editorial.   [2] Cf. *Jerusalem*, pp. 264 ff.

[3] Cf. de Zwaan in *H.T.R.* XVII, 2, 128; Windisch in *Beginnings of Christianity*, II, 338.

[4] The Western reviser was far too unintelligent to see this, and makes Silas stay at Antioch. Luke is not to be blamed if he credits his readers

man in the Temple contains nothing that cannot be paralleled from modern accounts of healings; we may hope that Ananias and Sapphira are legendary, but the story does not go beyond the bounds of psychological possibility. The summaries of miraculous activities at various points need not concern us, since it is inevitable that these would grow up if there were the smallest ground for them, or even none at all; but there is no reason to doubt that the grounds were considerable. Nor need we concern ourselves with Paul's conversion, in so far as the vision is concerned; the temporary blindness and its cure seem also within the bounds of reasonable probability.[1] Aeneas and Tabitha come from a stratum of tradition which is probably ancient, but looks very much like the kind of miraculous tradition which grows up quickly round a holy man, and has preserved the conventional forms of such traditions; no doubt Peter did work some remarkable cures while preaching in the country districts of Palestine, but we may well be dealing here with legends accepted by Luke in good faith. Cornelius on the other hand represents visions which are psychologically probable; the coincidence of Peter's vision with the arrival of Cornelius' messengers is the kind of coincidence which is easily invented, but has an awkward habit of occurring in real life. Peter's escape from prison has certainly acquired a number of legendary features, and miraculous escapes from prison are a regular theme of ancient religious literature.[2] But

[1] So Harnack, *Acts of the Apostles*, pp. 151 and 153. Why exactly he should admit that 'St Paul really lost his sight for a short while', but hold that the blinding of Elymas 'certainly did not occur in the way we are told' though it 'probably has some historical nucleus' I cannot imagine. The two blindings seem strictly on the same footing.

[2] The theme may go back to the *Bacchae* of Euripides, cf. Reitzenstein, *Hellenistische Wundererzählungen*, p. 121, where, however, the suggestion that the singing of Paul and Silas implies a magical hymn

it must be remembered that such escapes were probably easy to secure by bribery or influence, though they are no doubt often pious legends.

In the second half of Acts miracles also occur with some frequency. The case of Bar-Jesus has already been noticed. The summary of miracles at Iconium is treated by Harnack as evidence that it belongs to the first half of Acts, not to the second. This ignores the linguistic evidence, which would definitely class these chapters with the second half in respect of their use of specifically Lucan language; moreover the fact that we have this one summary of miraculous activities in the second half is more simply explained by the fact that it is a summary intended to be typical of all the Pauline missions. (Incidentally we have a more 'miraculous' summary of Paul's activities at Ephesus in xix. 11 ff.) The cripple at Lystra seems reasonable enough, as does the girl with a spirit of divination at Philippi; the escape of Paul and Silas from prison is suspicious, but in itself and apart from details which may be intended to enhance the miracle (e.g. xvi. 24) only involves a remarkable coincidence between the imprisonment and the earthquake. The summary of miracles at Ephesus and the incident of the 'sons of Sceva' are well within the bounds of credibility, although the text of the latter incident is extremely obscure.[1] It is particularly noticeable that it is not stated that Eutychus was killed as a result of his fall from the window; Luke may have regarded the incident as a miracle, but there is no evidence that he did so. The incident of the viper at Malta is a miracle if καθῆψεν means 'bit'; naturally we may, if we choose, suspect that the

similar to that in the Acts of Thomas is entirely unnecessary. Cf. *Hellenistic Elements*, p. 95 and the admirable discussion of the whole incident in *The Beginnings of Christianity*, IV, 196 f.

[1] For the text cf. *The Beginnings of Christianity*, IV, 240 f., and V, Additional Note 23.

viper was shaken off before it had time to bite, or alternatively that the miracle really happened; the cure of Publius's father is a miracle of a type that was no doubt reasonably common in the apostolic period, as it is in various religious movements of modern times.

Now we may suspect that the process of legendary accretion, inevitable in an age which expects miraculous cures and regards them as a vindication of theological truth, has already been at work on the stories of Acts. It would be rather strange if it were not so. But when we compare these miracles with those of the Apocryphal Acts we are conscious that we are moving in an entirely different world in which the wicked are blinded or struck dead, while the Apostle's disciples are raised to life more or less at the Apostle's whim. It is perhaps worth noting that the two miracles which are most suggestive of the Apocryphal Acts, the death of Ananias and Sapphira and the raising of Tabitha, both come from the early Palestinian traditions which centre round Peter. In both the Greek is distinctly semitic.[1] It is not to be supposed that Luke felt any difficulty about either story; but he has not recorded anything of the same kind in that part of the Gospel where he is drawing on his own recollections or where he could get first-hand information as to the facts of the Pauline missions.

We are now in a position to come to some conclusion as to the reliability of Acts as a historical narrative. Within its limits it appears to be high, but we must remember its limits. It sets out to describe the foundation of the Church at

---

[1] Acts v. 1–16 falls in the section for which de Zwaan accepts Torrey's theory of an Aramaic source. The construction is largely paratactic, though the parataxis has been modified by the simple expedient of putting a certain number of the verbs into participles. τί ὅτι appears twice in this section; elsewhere in Luke only in Lk. ii. 49; but this is to be ascribed to the LXX. For Tabitha cf. above, p. 30 f..

Jerusalem, which it does by the bodily insertion of the blocks of traditional matter, whether written or oral, which Luke was able to collect. With the death of Stephen we reach his real theme, the advance of the Gospel from Jerusalem to Rome. But until xi. 19 we have no guarantee of any chronological order; it is quite likely that Paul reached Damascus and found Christians there before Philip reached Samaria; and again that the Hellenist refugees reached Antioch before the conversion of Cornelius. But Samaria had to be evangelised before the Gentile world, and so Philip's visit to Samaria comes first; similarly Caesarea was nearer to Jerusalem than Antioch and so the first Gentile community is founded with the conversion of Cornelius. It is quite doubtful whether Luke had enough idea of the proper functions of a historian to realise the importance of dating his narratives; from his rather pretentious introduction to the Gospel story in iii. 1 we might suppose that he had. But his silence in Acts suggests the opposite. The famine-prophecy is by implication dated some time in the reign of Claudius; Herod's accession and death give two dates which were well known to his readers. Otherwise we are left to allusions to procurators and proconsuls whose tenures of office are by no means easy to establish and cannot have been easy for his readers to find out.[1] We cannot blame him for his failure to give dates in the opening chapters, since they were probably completely lost by the time he wrote; nor can we blame him for not recording them later, in view of his general purpose; but it is a serious limitation to his value as a historical source.

Another limitation which has been noticed is his preference

---

[1] A reader in Palestine might find it fairly easy to fix the dates of Felix and Festus, but not that of Gallio, and *vice versa*. But Josephus is no better in dating the procurators.

for dramatic incidents and miracles as against the routine life of the Church; but this again is part of his general scheme. It is curious that at Ephesus he only gives a rather disappointing summary of miracles, and the queer story of the sons of Sceva. But his main incident at Ephesus is the riot in the theatre, and it is possible that the Jewish exorcists and the sons of Sceva (who may or may not have been a Jew), and the first serious contact with pagan magic, possessed an importance at the time when Luke wrote, which led him to emphasise their defeat by the Gospel; the heresy implied in Colossians may well have included a good deal of syncretistic magic.[1] It is of course possible, as has been held by many, that Paul was imprisoned at Ephesus, as no doubt he was elsewhere; but there is no evidence whatsoever for the supposition. Undoubtedly Luke has omitted many of Paul's adventures, as is clear from 2 Cor. xi. 23 ff.; but it cannot be said that he has done so in order to prove the respectability of Christianity, since he has recorded quite enough of them to justify the objection of the authorities to the Church that it was a constant source of trouble.

Another limitation is his carelessness in compiling his sources. It would have saved a world of trouble if he had made it clear that the famine-visit of Paul and Barnabas to Jerusalem did not happen till after the death of Herod. But here again he is no worse than men who set out to be serious

---

[1] Cf. *Gentiles*, p. 149 ff. for an attempt to reconstruct the scheme of Paul's opponents. It must be remembered that the teachers of views of this kind would not have anything in the nature of a 'Creed' or 'system', and some may have been quite reputable philosophers while others may have been charlatans of the lowest type. It would not have occurred to any of them that Irenaeus's criticism (*Adv. Haer.* I, 14, 1,) ὅσοι γάρ εἰσι ταύτης τῆς γνώμης μυσταγωγοὶ τοσαῦται ἀπολυτρώσεις... was really a criticism at all: cf. below, p. 98.

historians.[1] Within these limitations he appears to be a truth-ful recorder of the facts available to him. He has chosen the form of a travel-story because the form appealed to the public taste and also probably to his own, but also because it suited the actual facts. The result is a very vivid and interesting narrative. In the speeches which he puts into the mouths of his characters he has given us a vivid picture of the faith of the early Church; we shall see that there is every reason to regard it as reliable.

[1] Thus he introduces Agabus in xxi. 10 as 'a certain prophet' though he has already appeared at xi. 28. But Josephus, (*B.J.* iii. 29) introduces Antioch as the capital of Syria and the third city in the Roman Empire with a complete disregard of the fact that he has already mentioned it thirteen times; he is simply starting a new source without revising it. Cf. also Antt. xix. 301 where Herod Agrippa I hears of a Gentile outrage on the synagogue at Dora, and protests against it to 'Publius Petronius, (now he was governor of Syria)'. But Petronius has already been the central figure of *Antt.* xviii. 261–309 as the governor responsible for carrying out Caligula's orders for the setting up of his statue in the temple.

CHAPTER V

THE THEOLOGY OF ACTS

We are now in a position to consider the theology which the author puts into the mouths of his characters, for it is mainly in the speeches that we get any guidance as to his knowledge of early Christian belief. Occasionally we meet with it in incidental remarks. We may further notice that in dealing with his theology we are not dealing with anything that professes to be a systematic exposition, and in consequence it is extremely dangerous to use the argument from silence. It is always a dangerous argument, but particularly so in dealing with a book such as Acts, especially if the author of Acts is also the author of Luke's Gospel. It has been well pointed out that if we possessed Acts alone we should suppose that the author took little interest in the history of the earthly ministry of Our Lord in view of the small number of allusions made to it in the Acts. We must further remember that the speeches have to be more or less in keeping with the supposed situation and character of the speaker.

We may begin with the general conception of God. In Paul's speeches at Lystra and Athens we find ourselves entirely on the conventional ground of Hellenistic Judaism. For the Judaism of the Dispersion it was axiomatic that the one God recognised by Gentile philosophy was the God of Israel revealed in the scriptures of the O.T. Now we know from Ro. i. 20 ff., that Paul was perfectly able and willing to use the conventional Jewish method of arguing from the best teaching of Gentile philosophers as to the unity of God and His perfect holiness, that Judaism was the true religion, in which that one God had revealed Himself; he even uses the argument of

Theophrastus (no doubt taken from a Jewish summary of Gentile philosophy) that it was the errors which invaded man's worship that had led him into a false idea of God's nature and so into sin.[1] At Lystra he uses the argument from the providential design of nature in language which almost suggests that Paul is paraphrasing a particular passage of Xenophon; this again he might quite well have known from some Jewish handbook of the opinions of the Greek philosophers in so far as they could be used for purposes of Jewish mission propaganda.[2] The quotation of Aratus at Athens is entirely in accordance with these methods, not least in the way in which the immanent deity of the Stoics is identified with the God of Israel revealed in the O.T.

These are the only two speeches in which Paul is represented as addressing Gentile audiences which have not been prepared by some kind of connection with the synagogue. It is of course possible that the speeches have been to some extent written up by Luke; but I am inclined to think that at least the reference to the 'Unknown God', probably drawn by a Jewish compiler from the guide-book curiosities of heathen religion, really served for Paul's text. We may note that 'vanity' or 'vanities' as a description of idolatry or particular false gods represented by idols is Pauline (Acts xiv. 15, cf. Ro. viii. 20 and i. 21), while 'allowing the Gentiles to walk in their own ways' is simply another way of saying that God 'handed them over to a reprobate mind'. The argument against idolatry as such in

---

[1] Cf. *Hellenistic Elements*, p. 32.

[2] The puzzling 'filling your hearts with food and gladness' is claimed by Torrey as an Aramaism, which seems unlikely. They look like a careless paraphrase of Xenophon, *Mem.* IV, iii. 5 f., where Socrates argues in favour of providence from the fact that man's need of food has been met by the provision of the fruits of the earth and suitable seasons which provide οὐ μόνον ὧν δεόμεθα ἀλλὰ καὶ ὧν εὐφραινόμεθα.

xvii. 29 is good Greek philosophical commonplace; the argument is frequent in hellenistic Judaism, as is the term τὸ θεῖον in the sense of God. It is appropriately put in Paul's mouth here, since he is concerned to deal with philosophers who would and often did object to the anthropomorphism of the Jewish religion.[1] We have no means of saying whether Paul would have used the term or not, since in his Epistles we have naturally no specimen of a direct approach to the pagan world. The specifically Christian conclusion to the speech on the Areopagus we shall consider later.

The doctrine of God in the other speeches in the book is naturally that presupposed in the O.T. The living God of Israel prepared the Jewish nation so that they might be His missionaries to the whole world. This is the theme of Stephen's speech, which is peculiar in its whole rejection of the history of Israel as a mistake from beginning to end. Judaism was of course in theory quite well aware of its missionary vocation. In Palestine indeed it is quite likely that communal friction between Jews and Gentiles had brought missionary work almost to a standstill, but the propaganda of the Dispersion was more or less at its high-water mark at this period. On the other hand the Jewish mission in general presupposed the acceptance by the Gentile convert of the commands of the Torah; the occasional exceptions whom we meet in Philo and Josephus seem to have been quite outside the main stream of orthodox Judaism. Stephen's speech appears to reflect the same feeling of the impossibility of converting the Gentile world to Judaism which we find in Paul. But it follows a quite different line of argument in rejecting the Torah; it is not that it has been fulfilled and superseded in the Gospel but

[1] Cf. Leisegang's index to the Cohn-Wendland text of Philo, *s. voc.* for Philo's use of the term and such passages as *Antt.* xx, 41 for Josephus's.

that from the beginning the Jewish nation has rejected the spirit in favour of the letter (cf. above, p. 23). Luke inserts the speech, but it must not be supposed that it is his own view: Paul's speech at Antioch deals with the question in a note appended by Luke to an older kerygma; to this we shall return later. To us Stephen's view and Paul's are quite incompatible; but to Jewish writers consistency meant little. Both Paul and Stephen held that Christ had put an end to the Torah. So long as they agreed on the main fact, the arguments by which they proved it were of secondary importance.

It was inevitable that in addressing Jews on the subject of the Gospel the Christian preacher should rely very largely on testimonies from the prophets and from the rest of the Old Testament. For it was agreed that God had prepared the world for a Messianic deliverance; the question was whether Jesus did or did not fulfil the role which the prophets had foreshadowed. This brings us to the second division of the doctrinal teaching of Acts, its Christology.

The primary prophecy on which the Church relied was that of Is. liii. It is possible that the suffering servant originally was a revised form of the conception of the Messiah; the saviour of Israel and of the world was not to be a conquering king but a persecuted prophet. It is further possible that there were even before Jesus circles in the Jewish nation which still interpreted the Messianic hope in this sense.[1] In any case Jesus interpreted

[1] For this point of view cf. Gressmann, *Der Messias*; it is doubtful whether full justice has yet been done to his views. In any case it should be noted that the absence of any idea of a suffering Messiah from rabbinical writings until a relatively late date is valueless as evidence of rabbinical, and still more of popular, beliefs at the time of the opening of the ministry of Jesus, since controversy with the Church would naturally lead to the suppression of anything that might seem to support the Christian view. It is at least remarkable that Paul's phrase in Col. i. 24 'I fill up what is lacking in the sufferings of Christ' is only intelligible in

it in this way[1] and it became the central argument of the Church in the appeal to prophecy. The use of the prophecy is common to all the more important N.T. writers, in spite of the fact that Paul uses it only once and then by implication rather than directly. The reason is not hard to see. For the use of the prophecy led to the use of the term 'The Righteous One' of Jesus, and in Jewish Christian circles 'righteousness' naturally carried with it the thought of the observance of the Torah, since it was in that that righteousness consisted. Paul's only use of the prophecy is in Ro. iv. 23 ff., a passage which has the air of a credal formula. It is implied in Luke xxiv. 26, John i. 29: Luke quotes it directly in Acts viii. 32 f.; cf. Matt. viii. 17, Heb. ix. 28, 1 Pet. ii, 21 f., Rev. v. 6, John xii. 38. It is implied in the title ὁ δίκαιος applied to Jesus in James v. 6, 1 John ii. 1 and *passim*: the title is applied to Jesus in Acts vii. 52 (Stephen) and xxii. 14 (Ananias), cf. iii. 14. (Cf. also 1 Clem. xvi. 2 ff. *Ep. Barn.* v. 2).[2]

In this respect Luke's emphasis on Is. liii. is in keeping with the rest of the N.T., a point which entitles us to suppose that he has preserved a picture which is generally reliable. In one

the light of a view which we first find on the authority of R. Acha (*c.* A.D. 320), though Paul introduces it as if it were quite a familiar idea. Cf. *Gentiles*, p. 167.

[1] I see no reason to doubt the authenticity of the saying of Mark x. 45.

[2] Cadbury, in *The Beginnings of Christianity*, v, 363, seems to fail entirely to do justice to the cumulative effect of these references as against Torrey. I am inclined to think that δίκαιος in Luke xxiii. 47 is not substituting a 'colourless "innocent" for the more technical or "superstitious" Son of God' but making the centurion an unconscious witness to Jesus as the Messiah. The prophecy could hardly be quoted more freely in view of Paul's reasons for avoiding it. The conception of the Messiah as 'the righteous one' appears in 1 En. xxxviii. 2: cf. Odes of Solomon xli. 13. Ps. Sol. xvii. 25, 28, 31 for righteousness as an attribute of the Messiah: in Ps. Sol. 'righteousness' is naturally the establishment of the Torah.

respect there is a notable omission. There is no hint of a Wisdom-Logos Christology such as Paul has developed as early as the writing of 1 Corinthians. On the other hand it must be remembered that such a Christology could only be expounded to an audience which had already accepted Jesus as the risen Lord of the Church and was also accustomed to the use made of the concepts of the divine Word or Wisdom by Hellenistic Judaism. Gentiles were of course accustomed to regard particular deities as manifestations of the divine Word or Wisdom which imposed order on the chaos of matter and animated both the world in general and the mind of man. But such deities were in general figures of a remote mythological era: deified emperors could indeed be given some of the attributes of a divine Logos, but such attributions were not taken seriously.[1] We have no scene in which Luke could have represented Paul as describing Jesus in this way with any approach to dramatic propriety, with the possible exception of his speech to the elders at Miletus: elsewhere he is addressing Jews or Gentiles whom he hopes to convert and to whom he can only give 'milk, not meat'.[2] In any case the doctrine could only have been introduced in xx. 18 ff. as a secondary matter: the point of the speech is to warn the reader, through Paul's lips, against the growing heresies of the primitive Church. (It is of course possible that Paul had already had occasion for such a warning and actually gave one on this occasion.)

On the other hand his one excursion into Christology before a Gentile audience, in the speech at Athens, is dramatically

---

[1] Cf. Nock, *Conversion*, pp. 236 f. For Nero as the head or animus of the Empire cf. *Gentiles*, p. 162. But this is merely the language of flattery.

[2] Acts xx. 28 cannot be taken as meaning 'with his own blood' but must mean 'the blood of his own' (ἰδίου = μονογενοῦς). Cf. *The Beginnings of Christianity*, IV, 262.

appropriate and thoroughly Pauline. Jesus is a man whom God has appointed: this fact is proved by his resurrection from the dead. This is precisely the Christology of Ro. i. 4, where Jesus is indeed the son of God, yet He has only been definitively appointed to that office by the spirit of sanctification as a result of His resurrection. Here the language is Jewish and intended to persuade the mainly Jewish readers to accept Jesus as the Messiah. But the thought of a man attaining to divinity and immortality as a result of his good deeds was familiar to Gentile readers.[1]

This Christology is not however confined to Paul; in Acts ii. 22 Jesus is a man appointed by God in order that God might work wonders through Him. God has raised Him from the dead because it was not possible for death to hold Him and has made Him both Lord and Christ (ii. 36). Here Peter is proving to a Jewish audience that Jesus is the Messiah. The proof lies in the Resurrection. It does not appear that there was any parallel in Jewish Messianic hopes for a death and resurrection of the Messiah in this form; at best there was a certain parallel in the belief that the Messiah would die at the end of the Messianic age and rise again with his saints (4 Esdr.

---

[1] Heracles was the notable example, his labours furnishing ample scope for the discovery of allegorical meanings. Cf. *Hellenistic Elements*, pp. 39 f.: to the references given there may be added Cicero, *De Fin.* III, xx, 66, Celsus *ap.* Orig. *c. Cels.* III, 22 (I, 218, 11), Plutarch, *Pelop.* xvi (286), Epict. *Diss.* II, xvi, 44. διὰ τοῦτο ἐπιστεύθη Διὸς υἱὸς εἶναι καὶ ἦν, Philo, *Leg. ad. G.* 81. Even the idea of a resurrection could find a certain analogy in Heracles's immortality attained from his death on Mt Œta. Cf. Diod. Sic. IV, xxxviii, 5, Seneca, *Herc. Œt.* 1940 ff. Here again the similarity was apparent rather than real in so far as Heracles, like Asclepius and the Dioscuri who figure in the same category, are figures of ancient mythology. Divine epiphanies in human form were more likely to gain credence as in Acts xiv. 11 f. Cf. Nock, *Conversion*, p. 90, and the curious version of the story of Medea and Pelias, Diod. Sic. IV, li, 1 ff.

vii. 27 ff.). But it might well be argued that the Resurrection of Jesus, if accepted, proved that the Church was right and Jewish expectations such as those of Ezra wrong. The inability of death to hold Jesus is due not to His divine nature but to the necessity of the fulfilment of the prophecies about Him. Thus we have here a tradition of a Christology similar to that of Paul according to which it was the fact of the Resurrection that made Jesus both 'Lord' and 'Christ'. The word 'Lord' was of course extremely vague; it could mean anything from the Jahweh of the O.T. in iv. 29 to a polite 'Sir' as in xvi. 30. Here it is a suitable title for Jesus as the exalted Lord of the Church, in whose name miracles are wrought and sins are forgiven. But it would be hard to say that it has any doctrinal implication, although in fact the Church in its attitude to Jesus has according to the picture drawn in these chapters of Acts already reached a position incompatible with the unitarian monotheism of Judaism.

We find a different Christology in Stephen's last words 'I see the heavens opened and the Son of Man standing on the right hand of God'. Here we have the same conception as in Mark xiv. 62. There have of course been many ingenious theories drawn from the resemblance between the Passion story of the Gospels and the martyrdom of Stephen, a resemblance which appears, though in a less striking form, between Luke xxiii. 34 and 46 on the one hand and Acts vii. 59, 60 on the other. It can be argued that Luke (or a copyist if we reject Luke xxiii. 34) has coloured the Passion-story with details drawn from that of Stephen;[1] it can equally be argued that the

---

[1] Creed *ad loc.* supports the omission of xxiii. 34 on the ground that 'so Christ-like a saying' could never have been omitted, and holds that its omission by B, D, W, Syr. Sin, etc. is right, the verse being a Marcionite insertion. But his argument ignores the anti-semitism of the primitive Church; a scribe who was familiar with Matt. xxvii. 25 would

story of Stephen has been coloured by details introduced from the story of the Passion, or that Stephen's actual last words have been preserved and that they were coloured by his knowledge of the story of the Passion. On these points there is a total absence of evidence which leaves a pleasing field open for speculation. But there is no evidence that Luke has been responsible for the introduction of any of these details; Stephen's vision of the heavens opened and the Son of Man standing on the right hand of God show more affinity with the Marcan story of the Passion than with the Lucan. On the other hand Acts vii. 59 f. look like a duplicate version of the story of Stephen's death which came to Luke by a separate line of tradition;[1] that tradition may of course have coloured the story of the Passion with details drawn from the story of Stephen or *vice versa*; but there is not a scrap of evidence. In any case the fact that Luke ascribes to Stephen the vision of the Son of Man standing on the right hand of God, while he has modified the corresponding Marcan picture in his passion-story suggests that he has here preserved intact a 'Son of Man' Christology which was current in the early Church for some time after the Resurrection though it has disappeared from the rest of the books of the N.T. outside the Gospels.

It is not until the conversion of Paul that we get anything which corresponds to the later and more developed Christology of the Pauline Epistles; here the risen Christ appears as an independent agent who reveals Himself to Paul, and sends him where he chooses, rather than as the man appointed by God to be the Messiah and to act as His agent. Even here there is a considerable heightening of the position of Jesus as between

feel it a duty to omit the verse. For in fact Jesus's prayer had not been answered; the fall of Jerusalem proved that the Jews had not been forgiven; cf. Origen's Hom. in Lib. Jesu Nave xxvi. 3 (vii. 462, 14, 31).

[1] Cf. above, p. 24.

ix. 5 and 10 ff. on the one hand and xxvi. 14 ff., in which He is
a far more independent agent, on the other. Yet again in xxii. 14,
in the speech addressed to the Jewish mob in the Temple, it is
the 'God of our fathers' who has appointed Paul to see Jesus
'the righteous one' and to preach Him to all men. Here it is
probable that Luke is writing with a sense of what is dramatically
appropriate. In any case we have merely a different shade of
emphasis, not a real difference of theology.

Here it seems we have a striking testimony to Luke's fidelity
to his sources and to their reliability. It is not for a moment to
be supposed that Luke believed that there had been an evolution
in the Christology of the primitive Church or even a development in the sense of Newman's famous doctrine of development. There had been a revelation of God in Jesus the Lord
and Christ, which the Church had accepted and the Jews had
rejected. Any language which expressed the central position
of Jesus as the Lord of the Church and the focus of its approach
to God, could properly be applied to Him; it was only in
contact with such specifically hellenistic perversions of the
Gospel as those which meet us in Colossians that this midrashic
expression of devotion was forced to crystallise into dogma.
Luke is writing after these controversies, and he has at one or
two points modified the actual tradition of the teaching of
Jesus to meet possible misinterpretations of that teaching.[1]
There is no suggestion that in Acts he has modified his sources
in order to make the Christology of the primitive community
harmonise with the later developments of Paul's theology,
though on his own general principles it would be hard to deny
that he had every right to do so.

This lends special interest to some of the terms applied to
Jesus in the early chapters of Acts. Thus he is the ἀρχηγὸς τῆς

---

[1] Cf. *Gentiles*, p. 149, n. 5.

ζωῆς in iii. 15 and an ἀρχηγὸς καὶ σωτήρ in v. 31. The title appears in Heb. ii. 10 and xii. 2, but nowhere else in the N.T. In Hebrews it looks as though the writer were aware of the term as an early title of Jesus which could be accommodated to his highly hellenistic point of view;[1] in Acts it looks more like a genuine reminiscence of a primitive way of speaking of Jesus as the Lord. Again Jesus as 'servant' of God looks primitive, and appears to come from Isaiah.[2] The term 'Saviour' is rare (v. 31 and xiii. 23), in both cases being used in its correct Jewish sense of the Messiah as the *goel* of the chosen people.[3] It is at least possible that in this use of the term we have an original Christian usage, in which Jesus was not a hellenistic saviour like the deified emperor, but a deliverer of his people of the Jewish type. The difference between Him and other

---

[1] In Heb. ii. 10 Jesus is the ἀρχηγὸς τῆς σωτηρίας (=ζωῆς); in xii. 2 he is the ἀρχηγὸς καὶ τελειωτής; for the hellenistic parallels, cf. *Hellenistic Elements*, p. 26: also for its possible reference to Jesus as the true ἀρχηγός of whom Joshua, the historical ἀρχηγός, is a type.

[2] Acts iii. 13 and iv. 27. The treatment of the subject in *The Beginnings of Christianity*, IV, 47 and V, 366, strikes me as unduly sceptical and to rest on a failure to recognise the extent to which the prophecy of Is. liii underlies the N.T. It is of course possible that the term was originally drawn from Is. xlii. 1 (cf. Matt. xii. 18) rather than Is. lii. 13. But the strand of prophecy could hardly be more freely used in the N.T. than it is, unless the authors are to be expected to reiterate the appeal to the same testimony an indefinite number of times. Cf. above, p. 73.

[3] 'Saviour' in the O.T. is a title normally reserved to Jahweh, but in Judges iii. 9 and 15 and Neh. ix. 27 is used of the judges as saviours of Israel; the judges are also ἀρχηγοί in some LXX versions of Judges v. 2 and 15, cf. xi. 6 and 11. An expectation of a Messiah of the type of the judges appears rather surprisingly in Philo, *de Pr. et Poen.* 95 (drawn from Num. xxiv. 7) in Philo's only lapse into Messianic expectations; he is at his most purely Jewish in this passage. The growing tension with Rome would naturally lead to hopes of 'saviours' of this kind at this period in Palestine. For the rabbinical view of the Messiah as *goel* cf. Str. B, 1, 68 f.; as restoring Israel to their own land, IV, 881 ff.

'saviours' was that He had come to deliver God's chosen people from their sins, not, as the false Christs promised, from the Roman oppressor.[1] The second of these instances comes in Paul's sermon at Antioch; it cannot be argued against the value of Luke's evidence that we have no parallel in the Pauline Epistles, since in this sort of usage we have no right to argue from Paul's silence; we have no Epistle which gives a specimen of his first address to a Jewish congregation. Moreover, the speech is simply a specimen of the early Christian kerygma; the allusion to Saul the son of Kish may be a reminiscence of Paul's habit of introducing his eponymous hero from the O.T., and the Pauline theology at the end is introduced to make it specifically Pauline, while it is possible that the omission of any reference to the synoptic story of the ministry of Jesus, as against the Petrine kerygma in x. 36 ff. represents an intentional modification by Luke of his source. But in itself the speech is a Christian interpretation of history as culminating in Jesus, and a collection of testimonies, proving that Jesus is the Christ; the quite unhellenised conception of the saviour here suggests that Luke is being faithful to good sources.[2]

We have then considerable justification for believing that Luke has left us an accurate picture of the theology of the early Church in Palestine and not simply read back into it the developed system of the Pauline period. His theology of the Holy Spirit is therefore likely also to go back to early sources. In considering it we may begin with his narrative of the day of

[1] It may be doubted whether Paul would have used the term in this sense; it only appears in the Epistles in Phil. iii. 20 where it is in the more hellenistic sense of a heavenly redeemer, adapted to the Jewish eschatological outlook. (Eph. v. 23 I cannot recognise as Pauline.)

[2] In Luke ii. 11 we have a far more hellenistic conception; the 'saviour' might be a Caesar. This does not prove anything as to Luke's sources here, since Judaism might quite well be influenced by the language of contemporary paganism. Luke i. 47 is purely the LXX usage.

Pentecost. Now there is no doubt that the story of Acts ii has been coloured by the belief that the coming of the Holy Ghost represented a new era in the history of the world. The nature-festivals of the early Hebrews had since the days of the prophets been transformed from their original meaning, in which they were all too liable to lead to syncretism with the local cults of the Baalim of the sanctuaries of Canaan, into commemorations of the mighty works of Jahweh in delivering his people from Egypt: the Passover had become a memorial of the Exodus, Tabernacles a memorial of how the people had lived in tents in the wilderness. Pentecost, as a harvest-festival, held out longest: Philo has no idea that it represents anything connected with the giving of the Torah. But between him and Luke the step has been taken; for Judaism Pentecost has become the feast of the giving of the Torah, and for the Church it is the day on which the new gift of the Holy Ghost replaces the Torah as God's supreme gift to man. This was by no means the only point of view. The tradition preserved by Matthew regarded the Sermon on the Mount as the new Torah, and the view is not simply Matthew's. For though he has increased the importance of the Sermon on the Mount by combining the comparatively short Sermon which is common to him and Luke with a large amount of other material, yet the shorter form of the Sermon, as Luke preserves it, would seem originally to have been a Sermon on the Mount. It is of course commonly referred to as the 'Sermon on the Plain' for the simple reason that Luke describes how Jesus chooses the Twelve on the top of a mountain after a night spent in prayer. He goes on to record that he came down and stood in a level place and delivered the Sermon. Now you do not take the trouble to record the fact that someone stood on a level place merely for its own sake: it is natural to stand on level places, exceptional to stand on mountains. The only reason for the mention of the level place would seem to be that Luke's source, described a Sermon on the Mount, and presumably regarded it as the giving of the new Torah: Luke altered it to a Sermon in a level place, apparently because the giving of the new Torah was reserved for Pentecost.

On the other hand the writing-up of Pentecost can hardly be the work of Luke himself; linguistically it is one of the passages where we have reason to suspect an Aramaic original;[1] as a story it is hopelessly confused. The Spirit descends in the form of tongues of fire on each of 'them', presumably the Twelve. This corresponds to the list of countries, which originally seems to have consisted of twelve, one for each Apostle. Thus each Apostle speaks in one strange tongue.[2] There should of course have been seventy nations of the world to hear the new Torah, and the source from which Luke derived the mission of the seventy, or more probably Luke

---

[1] οὐχὶ ἰδού in ii. 7 is accepted by de Zwaan as probably due to translation.

[2] As it stands there are fourteen, Egypt and the Cyrenaica being counted as one. Cretans and Arabians have been added by Luke himself or by a very early copyist, in deference to Paul's visit to Arabia and Titus's real or supposed mission to Crete (Titus i. 5). Although the letter is not genuine, it may quite well embody authentic information on this point. Titus is old enough to have contributed to the vocabulary of Ignatius; *Magn.* viii. 1 is a cento of Titus i. 14 and iii. 9, while κατα-στῆμα in *Trall.* iii. 2 is more likely to come from Titus ii. 3 than from Ignatius's astrological sources (Vett. Val. IV, 11; Kroll 175, 10). Thus the insertion may be older than A.D. 100, if it is not due to Luke himself; the silence of Acts as to such a mission is no evidence that Luke did not know of it. It might of course be argued that Titus has simply borrowed the idea of a mission to Crete from Acts. But the allusions to Crete here and in xxvii. 7 would hardly suggest Crete as the scene of a mission. Still it is probable that 'Cretes and Arabians' represent a very early insertion by some one who had read Titus and Galatians: if they are due to Luke we should expect him to mention Arabia at ix. 19.

himself, when he changed the Q story of the sending of the Twelve into a sending of the Seventy, was aware of the fact. Here, however, his source gave twelve nations, one for each Apostle, and he reproduced it with the possible addition of Cretes and Arabians, spoiling the numerical symmetry. But he went yet further in changing the original story. For the point of the story is that each nation heard in its own language. But Luke's scheme provides for the gradual spread of the Gospel from Jerusalem to Rome; and though he is aware of disciples at Damascus and Rome before the arrival of any mission which he records, it would spoil the whole of his scheme if the whole world had heard the Gospel on the day of Pentecost through its representatives, as it had heard the original giving of the Torah on Mount Sinai.[1] It would seem that it is Luke himself who is responsible for inserting the words 'Jews' in verse 5, with the result that we are asked to believe that devout Jews would need to hear the Gospel preached in the language of the countries in which they had been born; in reality it is most unlikely that any Jew of the Dispersion would have understood such native dialects as survived in the remoter regions of the Middle East, since the Jews of the Dispersion were almost entirely city dwellers. The original version described the promulgation of the new Torah to the nations of the world through their representatives, the proselytes who happened to be in Jerusalem for the feast. It may indeed be doubted whether many proselytes would have understood these dialects, but there would be distinctly less improbability in their case. In fact Greek, Latin and two dialects of Aramaic would have been quite adequate for the whole of the supposed audience, whether Jews or proselytes. It may be added that the list is one of the purely conventional descriptions of the wide diffusion of

[1] Cf. *Judaism*, I, 276f.

Judaism which are a favourite theme with Jewish writers of the
period. They were themselves modelled on similar lists of the
countries subject to the power of the Roman empire in vogue
among heathen writers.[1]

Thus the original story of Pentecost was a proclamation of
the new Torah to the proselytes of all the world as viewed by
a Jew of Jerusalem, probably by origin a Jew of the Dispersion.
There is no reason to doubt that there was some initial outpouring of the Holy Ghost in the form of a speaking with
tongues and there is no reason to suppose that it did not occur
on the day of Pentecost after the Resurrection; the identification
of the first coming of the Holy Ghost with the giving of the
new Torah is more easily explained if it rests on a historical
coincidence.

The speech of Peter recorded in Acts consists of a bare
summary of the primitive kerygma, combined with a selection
of testimonies. Joel had foretold the outpouring of a gift of
prophecy immediately before the coming of the great and
notable day of the Lord. In Jesus the messianic promises had
been fulfilled; His resurrection was the event foretold in the
sixteenth Psalm, a Psalm which could not refer to David but
must refer to his promised successor, the Messiah. Jesus had

---

[1] For Jewish lists of this kind cf. Philo, *Leg. ad* G. 281 ff., in Flacc.
45 ff. Schürer, *G.J.V.* III, 5, treats these statements as if they could be
relied on as evidence. No doubt the Jewish dispersion was enormous;
but Philo, *Leg. ad* G. 10, from a pagan source shows the models from
which these descriptions are derived. Jos. *B.J.* II, 362 ff. gives a
full-length picture of the Roman Empire and legions in this vein;
cf. Aelius Aristides's 'panegyric' of Rome (Keil XXIV (XIV), 91 ff.).

Even if any proselytes knew the dialects of their native places, they
would have to be bilingual in order to understand the synagogue service,
which would be in Greek or Aramaic, except for those parts which were
still read in Hebrew with an Aramaic Targum in Palestine and the
Eastern Diaspora.

been raised from the dead and exalted to the right hand of God; having been so exalted he had received the promised gift of the Holy Ghost which had just been manifested. Here there is a gap in the argument; why had Jesus received this gift and poured it out on His disciples? The answer is that Luke was not well enough versed in rabbinical theology to appreciate an allusion which in his sources was probably made clearer. In the sixty-eighth Psalm we read: 'Thou hast gone up on high, thou hast led captivity captive, thou hast given gifts unto men' or 'received gifts for men'. 'Leading captivity captive' no doubt originally meant that the conqueror to whom the hymn was addressed had led his prisoners through Jerusalem to the Temple or to some other suitable centre of his triumph. But it could quite well mean 'Thou hast won a glorious prize' after the going up already referred to. Now the Psalm is a Psalm for Pentecost in the modern Jewish prayer-book, as it is in the Anglican, which here follows the Roman breviary. The rabbinical exegesis of the Psalm was that the verse referred to Moses, who was taken up to heaven to receive the Torah; on his arrival the angels so objected to his being given anything so precious as the Torah that they cried out in disgust 'Lord, what is man that thou art mindful of him, and the son of man that thou visitest him?' It was not until Moses at God's instruction had referred them to Exod. xx. 2, with its reference to the house of bondage and its prohibition of idolatry, that he was able to convince them that the Torah was not meant for them but for man. So Moses, having ascended, won his prize, the Torah, and brought it back as a gift for men. The Targum on that Psalm interpreted the verse 'The Lord gave the word; great was the company of the preachers' by the rendering 'Thou by thy word gavest thy word unto thy servants the prophets.' So Jesus, having been exalted to the right hand of God, received from the Father the promised Spirit, and has poured it out on His Apostles.[1] In the light of the rabbinical view the whole conception becomes clear, whereas in Acts, as it stands, there is no clear explanation of the reason why the exaltation of Jesus to heaven should be followed by the sending of the Holy Spirit. Luke's source was no doubt aware of the appropriateness of the Psalm in view of the rabbinical interpretation, and I suspect that we have in it evidence that the Psalm in question was already a Psalm for Pentecost in the Jewish liturgy. The thought might indeed be Pauline; it is fully developed in Eph. iv. 8. But it may well be older than Paul: it is also implied in the saying in John. vii. 39 that the Spirit was not yet, because Jesus was not yet glorified.[2] Luke's failure to see the point and to produce the testimony here shows that we are dealing with material which came to him in a tradition which was not that of the Pauline Churches.[3] Nor is it hard to see why the conception should not appear in the genuine Pauline writings. The devout proselytes of the source, whom Luke has changed into Jews, no doubt regarded the sending of the Holy Ghost as the giving of the new Torah, written on the tables of the heart; but that need not imply that those who had received the gift of the Holy Spirit were dispensed from observing the letter. Jesus had not come to destroy but to fulfil.[4]

[1] The story of the debate between God, the angels and Moses is of course to be regarded as a rabbinical conceit; the conception of the Torah as a heavenly treasure entrusted to Moses for Israel is entirely serious. For the rabbinical exegesis cf. Str. B on Eph. iv. 8.

[2] Cf. John xiv. 16, xv. 26, xvi. 13.

[3] The writer of Ephesians has a remarkable grasp of Pauline theology, but there is no reason to suppose that he derived it from personal acquaintance rather than from the corpus of Pauline Epistles. This particular point may well be non-Pauline.

[4] A writer with Matthew's semitic mentality would see no difficulty in regarding both the Sermon on the Mount and the day of Pentecost as

This conception of the day of Pentecost as the new Sinai does not meet us elsewhere in the Acts. The Holy Ghost becomes a gift of power which enables the Apostles to speak with all boldness and to vindicate their claim to speak with divine authority by the working of miracles (iv. 29 f.); the power is extended to Stephen (vi. 8 and 10). In the case of Stephen we have the same conception as in Luke xxi. 15, where Jesus promises to give His disciples a mouth and wisdom which their opponents will be unable to resist, preserving an earlier form of the saying than Mark xiii. 11.[1] Even where the Holy Ghost is the power residing in the Church, which enables the Apostles to act with the assurance that what they bind on earth will be bound in heaven, His action is normally of a miraculous character. Ananias and Sapphira lie to the Holy Ghost with disastrous results to themselves: the descent of the Spirit is a visible proof that Samaritans can be admitted to the Church and again that Cornelius and his friends, though uncircumcised, are capable of receiving baptism. It is not clear how far a visible gift of the Spirit, in the form of speaking with tongues or some similar manifestation, always accompanies baptism. Ananias in ix. 17 is sent to baptise Paul that he may recover his sight and be filled with 'holy spirit'; he recovers, but we are not told of a coming of the Holy Ghost, though nothing can be inferred from Luke's silence. It might seem from xix. 2

the giving of the new Torah; if he had wanted to be consistent, he could have represented the former as the promulgation of the Torah, the latter as the giving of the power to keep it. Luke may have been enough of a hellenist to feel that it was inconsistent to have two givings of a new Torah, while for Paul and his immediate circle it was impossible to admit that the sermon was a new Torah without making it possible for Jewish Christians to hold that the new Torah had merely extended the obligations of the old, but not abolished its literal observance. It is possible that Paul has such a view in mind in Gal. v. 13 ff.

[1] I owe this point to Prof. C. H. Dodd. But the two conceptions are identical in Acts, cf. v. 32.

that Paul expects it when he asks the disciples of John whether they received the Holy Ghost when they were baptised; but this need not be implied. Paul finds a little coterie of Jews (he is still working in the synagogue) with peculiar Messianic views; he assumes that they are Christians and puts his question as a matter of interest; it is only when they say that they have heard nothing of the Holy Ghost that he discovers that they are disciples of John, not of Jesus; his action in baptising them is again vindicated by a glossolaly.[1]

In the early chapters the Holy Ghost is manifested mainly in this thaumaturgic form, which vindicates the truth of the Gospel and the authority of the Apostles to preach it. Jesus Himself had refused to give signs from Heaven, but the primitive Church was quite unable to resist the temptation to use the miracles, which are a normal accompaniment of an outburst of religious enthusiasm in an atmosphere in which miracles are expected, as evidence for the truth of the particular doctrinal system which underlies the outburst of enthusiasm, or of the divine authority of the person or persons round whom it centres. This is particularly strongly expressed in Acts iv. 30, where the primary function of the Holy Ghost appears to be the production of miraculous cures; but the same conception underlies the account of the ministry of Jesus in the Fourth

---

[1] The disciples of John have given rise to innumerable conjectures; it can only be said that there is a total lack of evidence. Here the Ephesian disciples form a little group within the synagogue; there is no mention of such a group in the case of Apollos, who simply appears in the synagogue, presumably with an urgent message of repentance. The twelve of Acts xix. 7 constitute a group of some kind, but we cannot argue from them to an organised Johannine 'Church' (surviving perhaps in the Mandeans). The Mandeans appear to have no connection with the Baptist apart from their own imagination (cf. Brandt in *E.R.E.* VIII. 390 f.). Outside Palestine the Baptist's movement was far more likely to produce small coteries within the synagogue than a 'Church'.

Gospel (cf. especially John xii. 37) and Heb. ii. 4. It is noticeably absent from 1 Peter and the Pastorals: the initial 'enthusiasm' is giving way to settled order. In Paul it appears in Gal. iii. 5: but here Paul is hard put to it to argue with his Jewish opponents; here it is God who supplies the Spirit and works wonders; in Ro. xv. 18 it is Christ who vindicates Paul's message by working wonders through him. But it is to be observed that in both these cases Paul is writing primarily for Jewish readers or readers who are under the influence of Judaism; even in Gal. v. 13 ff. the work of the Spirit is described in ethical terms, while in 1 Cor. xii. and xiii. the miraculous side of the action of the Spirit is reduced to the minimum; His function is to provide for the government of the Church and to confer the gifts of faith, hope and charity on the individual. The change is of course due to the fact that manifestations of the Spirit, perhaps including miracles, are being produced at Corinth without regard to the observance of order in the worship of the Church, perhaps without regard to the elementary demands of Christian conduct; it is at least possible that those who prided themselves on being πνευματικοί were also proud of their freedom from the burden of external moral rules in regard to sexual matters.[1]

In the later chapters of Acts we find that the action of the

---

[1] Origen, c. Cels. II, 51 (1, 173, 20 ff.) appears to be the first Christian to recognise that miracles as such prove nothing; it is only where they produce, or are accompanied by, growth in holiness that we have evidence that they are due to the power of God, not to magic or demons. On the other hand, if a creed or movement produces a growth in holiness, it does not appear why miracles are needed. It should be noted that, while the Fourth Gospel in general takes an entirely thaumaturgic view of miracles, in the story of the Centurion's son (iv. 48) we have the Synoptic point of view: yet in Matt. and Luke there is no parallel to this verse. This tells strongly in favour of the view that the writer's synoptic material is drawn from a different line of tradition from Mark and Q.

Holy Spirit is modified. The subject-matter does not call for allusion to the ethical fruits of the Spirit; but the action of the Spirit mainly takes the form of a prophetic inspiration, guiding Paul in his actions (xvi. 6 f., xix. 21, xx. 23) or inspiring prophets (xi. 28, xxi. 11). The prophecies are of course divinely inspired, but there is nothing miraculous about them. The prophecy of Agabus was part of a general prophecy of the portents which would usher in the second coming of the Lord; it was fulfilled in a quite severe famine which rendered the help of the Antiochene converts highly opportune (cf. above p. 35). The other warnings and prophecies were fairly obvious forebodings of the probable result of a visit paid by Paul to Jerusalem.

Thus individual inspiration and sanctification are emphasised and the thaumaturgic aspect of the action of the Spirit declines in the later chapters. The same may be said of his action on the Church as a body. We have a curious instance in xiii. 2, where the leaders of the Church of Antioch are fasting and worshipping; the Holy Ghost orders them, apparently quite suddenly, to separate Paul and Barnabas for some particular work; the result is the first missionary journey. I see no reason to modify the view I have put forward elsewhere that this call is the result of the conflict between Peter and Paul at Antioch.[1] Here we have a special corporate guidance of the Church, though presumably it began with the inspiration of an individual, accepted by the rest as a divine call.[2] An even more

[1] *Jerusalem*, pp. 193 ff. The description of the circumstances suggests that guidance was being sought in some special crisis; psychologically the sense of an overpowering call to such work is more easily intelligible if it was evoked by a situation demanding action of some kind.

[2] The situation is that of 1 Cor. v. 3 ff., except that Paul has already made up his mind; the action is ascribed to 'the power of Our Lord Jesus Christ' rather than to the Holy Ghost, probably to avoid the awkwardness of a reference to the Spirit in the same context as a description of Paul himself as 'present in the spirit though absent in the body'.

remarkable conception is implied in the startling claim of the Council of Jerusalem that 'it seemed good to the Holy Ghost and to us' in xv. 28 (cf. above, p. 50). We find a similar conception in xx. 28, where the Holy Ghost has appointed the elders of the Church who meet Paul at Miletus, but here the expression is made easier by the fact that appointment to office in the Church was a ministry conferred by the Spirit (1 Cor. xii. 28). Whether ordination was necessary at this period of history as the means of conveying the gift of the Spirit for the work of the ministry is one of the many problems on which there is a total lack of evidence.

Thus we have a steady reduction of the emphasis on the miraculous aspect of the working of the Spirit which corresponds to the development in the Pauline Epistles; it seems reasonable to suppose that Luke is here reproducing his sources faithfully; whether the earlier sources exaggerated or not is another matter.[1]

[1] Harnack (*Acts of the Apostles*, p. 141) distinguishes between the we-sections and the rest of the latter half of Acts; in the we-sections we have 'no less than fourteen instances of a miraculous character' in about 100 verses; in the rest we have only ten, which can be reduced to six in view of the fact that the action of the Spirit in xx. 23 and 28 is in a recorded speech of Paul, the earthquake at Philippi is a natural coincidence, not a miracle, while xxviii. 25 is simply a normal way of introducing an O.T. quotation. He proceeds to reduce the six left by claiming that xviii. 9 f. and xxiii. 11 are 'out of organic connection with the simple narratives in which they stand and give the impression of having been thrust into the context'. There is no reason to suppose that there was anything miraculous in these passages; such internal monitions are common; the extent to which they take the form of 'visual hallucinations' which may, or may not, be genuine visions is a matter of temperament. It is true that xviii. 9 f. and xxiii. 11 can be cut out without loss to the sense; so can xviii. 5, 7, 8, 17 and 23. Luke's narrative style allows the excision of almost any incident. The relative frequency of prophecies, etc. in the we-sections is simply due to the more detailed character of the narrative.

Theologically the position of the Holy Ghost in the Christian scheme is entirely undefined. At times, as in xv. 28, we have an almost complete personification. We find a similar personification in rabbinical Jewish writing, resembling that of Wisdom in the Wisdom literature. It goes without saying that such personifications in Judaism are merely a literary form. On the other hand it is doubtful whether any Jewish writer could have used the phrase in the sense of xv. 28; we seem already to have reached a view of the Holy Ghost approximating to that of later Trinitarian theology, as we do also in such Pauline passages as 1 Cor. xii. 11 and 2 Cor. xiii. 13. Elsewhere as in xvi. 6 the Spirit need mean no more than an act of divine guidance. It would seem that Acts reflects the gradual and quite unrationalised development by which the relation of the Spirit to God in Himself and to Jesus as the exalted Christ is passing from its purely Jewish form of belief in a spiritual action of God or the Lord on the mind and soul of the disciple into the later Christian conception of a 'person' within the divine Trinity. His relation to God and to Christ seems to be completely vague and undetermined.

Angels appear frequently in the first half of Acts; in the second they appear as active agents only in St Paul's words at xxvii. 23. In the first half they are mentioned eighteen times, of which four are in Stephen's speech, replacing theophanies of the O.T. At v. 19 an angel delivers 'the Apostles' from prison and Peter's deliverance and Herod's death account for seven references. At viii. 26 an angel orders Philip to go and meet the Ethiopian; but somewhat remarkably 'the spirit of the Lord' carries him away at the end of the incident. Probably here the language has been influenced by the O.T. (2 Kings ii. 16), but we may simply have a stylistic change by Luke or a chance variation of phrase in his source. Of the rest four come in the incident of Cornelius; the number might be counted as five since the man in bright raiment at x. 30 is simply a way of describing an angel.

Now it is interesting to observe how small a part angels play in the Pauline Epistles. There are only three passages in which they are quite unequivocally good, Gal. i. 8 (where the point lies in the absurdity of the supposition), iv. 14 and 2 Thess. i. 7 in a piece of purely conventional Jewish apocalyptic. Elsewhere they tend to be treated with no great respect,[1] though it is not for a moment to be supposed that Paul doubted that God employed angelic messengers to communicate His will to men, and that many at least of them had passed successfully through their time of probation. But it would seem that he normally thought of God as communicating with men, or at any rate with His chosen servants, through the Spirit in the form of an overwhelming sense of spiritual constraint or through visions. The angelic vision of xxvii. 23 f. may in that case be his way of describing a communication to the heathen ship's company;[2] the hearers may then have understood him to mean a divine messenger rather than a Jewish-Christian 'angel'.

Once again it looks as though Luke had reproduced his sources with remarkable fidelity. It seems that he would naturally talk of the Spirit as God's method of conveying His will to man, but that he would ascribe such messages to the mediation of angels without any hesitation where his sources did so. He could obviously have written up the story of the deliverance of Paul and Silas at Philippi on the lines of Peter's

---

[1] Cf. Kittel in *T.W.z.N.T.*, *s.voc.* (i, 84 f.).

[2] Messenger-gods are well known in Greek religion (cf. Kittel, *loc. cit.*); but angels as intermediaries between gods and men seem to come into paganism only under Jewish or Christian influence, which would not be likely to have affected Paul's hearers. But Paul might well have used (or be appropriately represented as using) the term without troubling to ask precisely how his hearers would understand it.

deliverance from Herod, or written down the story of Peter's deliverance on the lines of that of Paul and Silas, but he has not done so. Here, as elsewhere, we find a difference in Luke's picture of the religion of primitive and Pauline Christianity which is confirmed by the Pauline Epistles on the one hand and the general outlook of the synoptic Gospels as to angels and by the frequent allusions to them in apocalyptic Jewish literature on the other.[1]

With regard to Paul's special theological views it has been objected that Luke's exposition of them in Acts xiii. 16 ff. is so slight as to prove that he knew little of them or did not understand them.[2] This fails to recognise either the nature of the speech, as a specimen kerygma, or Luke's sense of dramatic fitness. The original probably had nothing specifically Pauline about it. On the other hand Paul could not conceivably intro-

[1] For angels in apocalyptic and rabbinical literature cf. *Judaism*, I, 401 ff. Philo preserves angels, but usually as divine *Logoi* or as the higher order of Platonic souls which from time to time appear as men and then revert to their former state (*De Gig.* 12, following *Phaedo* 69 c); we have an orthodox Jewish view in such passages as *De Abr.* 113 ff., where Philo is following a source which represents the normal Jewish *haggada*. Paul's attitude is peculiar in so far as they are to be judged by the Saints in 1 Cor. vi. 3 and still liable to temptation (*ibid.* xi, 10). This may be due to the fact that they are fitted into the astrological world-scheme which he employs in Ro. viii. 38; they may at the same time be the angels of the nations of the world.

[2] Cf. Windisch in *The Beginnings of Christianity*, II, 337. His criticism that it is a misunderstanding of Paulinism since 'faith seems to be a supplement of strict observance of the Law' seems to be a complete misunderstanding of xiii. 38. Emmet, *op. cit.* p. 295 remarks that this interpretation is not certain, 'and even if this be the meaning, it might be a contemporary's misconception of Paul's difficult and subtle doctrine'. I should prefer to say that while it is possible to force this meaning upon the words it is a quite unnatural interpretation; the natural sense is that the Law of Moses could not bring any justification from sin, while all who believe in Jesus are justified.

duce his whole conception of the abolition of the Torah as a result of the new dispensation in his first address to a synagogue; he could at most drop a hint of it of a kind which might appeal to Gentile hearers without raising a riot among Jewish members of the congregation. To expound the whole of his system adequately Paul would have needed to reason 'from morning to evening', as he does at Rome. It may be doubted whether in fact Paul could do more at a first sermon in any place than prove from the prophets that Jesus was the Messiah; Luke introduces verses 38 f. as a kind of postscript to make his specimen kerygma include the specifically Pauline version of the Gospel. As a matter of fact his introduction of the testimony of Hab. i. 5 is dramatically inappropriate to the occasion; it could only give offence to a synagogue audience at this point and could only be used with effect when it was clear that the Jewish hearers had more or less decided to reject the Gospel. It is simply a testimony against the Jews, and no doubt Paul used in on occasion; but at the end of his first address it would certainly be premature.[1]

It may be noted that Luke uses the occasion for introducing by implication several of the main Pauline doctrines. In xiii. 43 the converted Jews and proselytes are encouraged to 'adhere to the grace of God', in verse 48 'all who were ordained to eternal life' believe; in xiv. 3 the Lord bears witness 'to the word of His grace' by signs and wonders. We are thus given a summary of Paul's teaching in relation to Judaism on the occasion of the first visit to a Gentile city which Luke describes in detail. The remaining speeches in Acts are specimens of Paul's preaching to Gentile or Christian audiences; here his views on justification by faith, grace and predestination vanish or take a secondary

[1] The statement that 'almost the whole city' came together to hear Paul on the next sabbath is a conventional exaggeration, cf. Posid. ap. Athenaeus, *Deipn.* v, xlviii, 212 *b*.

place, as they do in the Epistles, apart from Galatians and Romans. It must be remembered that Paul was not a Calvinist, but a hellenistic Jew, ready to use any argument to advance his one purpose, the conversion of the Gentiles, and determined to abolish the observance of the Law, the supreme obstacle in his path. The space occupied by his doctrine of justification by faith in the Epistles is due to the fact that two are entirely devoted to his rejection of the Torah. His speech at Miletus contains indeed some echoes of the earlier Epistles, such as 'the Gospel of the grace of God' (xx. 24) and 'the word of His grace' (verse 32), as well as a defence against the charge of 'pleasing men' by not preaching the whole Gospel (verses 26 f., cf. Gal. i. 10), and a reference to Paul's practice of working for his living (verses 34 f.). Thus it covers by implication several of the points raised in the Epistles; if Luke did not know the Epistles, he seems quite familiar with the situation implied in them. But in the main the speech looks forward to the new danger which had appeared at Corinth and was appearing at Colossae. That danger was the rise of popular teachers claiming 'spiritual' gifts of a special order; in virtue of their special character they would produce new versions of the Gospel, which could only end in breaking the Church up into conventicles.

With the rest of Paul's theology, as expounded in his speeches I deal elsewhere (cf. above, pp. 27 f. and 69). His attitude towards Judaism as described by Luke has been said to be completely inconsistent with that of the Epistles; I can only say that the charge appears to show a complete failure to understand Paul's attitude towards the religion of his fathers. He was quite prepared to remain a Jew and a Pharisee, so far as his own way of life was concerned; he would seem to have held that Judaism was binding on Jewish Christians, at least for the sake of peace, if not as a matter of absolute obligation.

Naturally this had to be modified in so far as such matters as eating with Gentile converts were concerned; but then in Paul's view Gentile Christians were ritually free from defilement and therefore the rules by which Judaism sought to avoid defilement arising from contact with the Gentiles did not apply in their case. We have in Acts no systematic exposition of Paul's theology; but it was not part of Luke's scheme to write a manual of dogmatic theology as expounded by his teacher, but to write an account of his travels, in which his expositions of the Gospel were introduced at appropriate points. His readers could be presumed to be familiar with the general outlook of the Churches Paul had founded, and probably with his epistles; there was no need to cover the same ground again. Within his limits Luke gives a good exposition of Paul's doctrinal position, all the better in that he does not over-emphasise that particular aspect of it which dominates Galatians and Romans and disappears from the rest of the Pauline Epistles.[1]

It is of course disappointing that apart from the controversy with Judaism Luke gives us no information as to the various perversions of the Gospel which figure in the Pauline Epistles. Yet he can hardly be blamed for his failure. It is completely

[1] It has been objected that Paul could not possibly have described himself as a Pharisee in xxiii. 6; either we must suppose him to have been grossly dishonest or else Luke shows a complete ignorance both of Paul and of Pharisaism (Windisch, *Beginnings of Christianity*, II, 333; his view is rightly rejected by the editors in the commentary in vol. IV *ad loc.*). It would be strange if Luke was so ignorant of the situation that he could represent Paul as speaking to this effect in xxiii. 6, and yet sufficiently aware of it to make Paul feel some doubts as to the justifiability of his action in using the words in xxiv. 21. There was always hope that the Pharisees on the Sanhedrin would realise that they had more in common with Christianity than with the entirely worldly view of the Jewish religion held by the Sadducees. That the Pharisees should have upheld Paul on this occasion against the Sadducees is not in the least surprising to any one with any knowledge of ecclesiastical politics.

misleading to describe such perversions as 'heresies', since the term suggests a more or less organised movement with a more or less coherent and consistent doctrinal system, seeking to impose its beliefs on the Church as a whole, and in the last resort claiming to be the only true Church. It has already been noticed that the conception of a Church was entirely alien to the hellenistic world (cf. above, p. 48). The danger that threatened primitive Christianity after the failure of the attempt to limit it to Jews and proselytes was not the capture of the Church as a whole by an organised movement, but rather the dissolution of the local churches, by the teaching of leaders who did not feel in any way bound to preserve the original Gospel, into little cliques in which there was no room for the ordinary Christian. Their 'spiritual' gifts might take the form of exaggerated asceticism, Gnostic speculation, antinomianism or apocalyptic expectation or some variation of Judaism. Their common feature was their refusal to recognise the Church as a world-wide Body of Christ, inheriting the ancient privileges of Judaism, and to substitute for it the local clique composed of the admirers and followers of a leader who was under no obligation to accept the faith or discipline of the Church.[1] To

[1] For groups of πνευματικοί forming themselves outside or on the fringe of the Church of the ψυχικοί, and refusing to recognise the bishops or clergy owing to their spiritual inferiority cf. Reitzenstein, *Historia Monachorum*, pp. 185 ff. He rightly points out that the 'Gnostic' heresies described by Irenaeus do not attempt to form 'Churches': there is no evidence of such an attempt before Marcion. The opponents of Ignatius are quite unidentifiable if we assume that the various 'heresies' of his time were 'systems' of teaching with fixed creeds and organisations. In *Trall.* v we seem to have an astrological gnosticism: Ignatius can claim to know as much about it as his opponents. In *Magn.* viii we have a tendency to judaise (cf. *Philad.* vi), in *Smyrn.* v ff. Docetics. The references in *Eph.* vii ff. are too general to allow of classification. Ignatius's zeal for the episcopate is due not to its being a novelty, but to the fact that it is the only bond of unity between local churches and in each local

describe the various 'systems' of such teachers would have involved writing a book on the scale of the first book of Irenaeus's work against the heresies. It is indeed quite probable that Luke was not very well acquainted with their views and it is quite uncertain how wide their influence was when Luke wrote; it is a pity that he has not given us more information, but it is quite probable that at the time he did not realise how serious their influence was going to be in the next hundred years. Even the greatest of historians cannot be criticised for failing to forsee the future.

church itself against the disruptive tendencies of those who claim to be πνευματικοί. Cf. the false prophet of Hermas, *Mand.* xi. In the N.T. we have an encratite form of asceticism in 1 Tim. iv. 1 ff. Hymenæus and Alexander in i. 20 may be teachers who go to the opposite extreme, but may simply be prominent Christians who have lapsed into sin. The charge of taking money in vi. 5 is common form: it may have been true in many cases, but was pretty certain to be made. In 2 Tim. ii. 14 ff. Hymenæus and Philetus look like Gnostics who claim to be already completely 'spiritual' as having risen to a new life (the logomachies and βεβήλοι κενοφωνίαι suggest a system influenced by hellenistic theologies, cf. verse 23). There is a lively picture of their methods in 2 Tim. iii. 6 ff. In Tit. i. 10 we have similar methods used by teachers who are to some extent judaisers. In Heb. x. 25 we have a warning against forsaking the ἐπισυναγωγὴ ἑαυτῶν, as some do, coupled with an injunction to provoke one another to love and good works. The later statement that marriage is honourable (xiii. 4) and the warning against strange teachings which try to establish the heart 'with meats' and not 'with grace', followed by an insistence on the Eucharist as the Christian sacrifice indicates a tendency on the part of some Christians to separate themselves on the basis of a more advanced asceticism. 1 Tim. i. 4 ff. suggests a form of Judaism: the writer is however so muddleheaded that it is impossible to say what form of error (if any) he had in mind. It is not clear how far we have in these cases a desire to revert to Judaism and the synagogue, the desire to form a Jewish-Christian group on the borders of the Church, or some combination of Christianity with an unidentified form of Jewish Gnosticism.

7-2

APPENDIX

Differences of language in Luke and Acts (see p. 14, n. 2.)

The instances which Clark regards as most important are discussed
above. The remainder are dealt with here for the sake of complete-
ness; it may be said at once that they are equally unconvincing. On
p. 398 f. he gives a list of agreements between Luke, Acts and Paul
with Hebrews), intended to show that in many cases the frequency
with which Luke and Acts use the same word differs so widely that
their common use of it proves nothing. In this list there are two
cases where there is a fairly wide divergence between Luke and Acts.
Thus τις attached to a noun is found thirty-three times in Luke,
seventy times in Acts. But the subject and style of Acts are always
introducing 'a certain' Jew, disciple or what not; the Gospel does
not do this to nearly the same extent. In twenty-seven cases the
Gospel uses τις with a noun to introduce a new character or scene. In
the first half of Acts we have thirteen such cases, in the last half
thirty. Of the remaining cases in Acts, six are used as a measure of
time in such phrases as 'certain days' which do not occur in the
Gospels. Since Matthew and Mark only use the form of expression
three times each the agreement between the Gospel and the Acts is
more impressive than might appear at first sight. ὑπάρχειν (Luke
seven, Acts twenty-six) looks significant on the surface. It seems
that Clark does not include the phrase τὰ ὑπάρχοντα 'possessions',
since he gives none for Matt. who uses this term four times. But if
so the uses of the verb to mean 'belong' should be ignored also.
This gives the word seven times in Luke, seven times in Acts i–xii,
fourteen times in Acts xiii–end. Of the seven times in Luke, four
come in Lucan passages, and three in Luke's revision of his sources.
Clark gives next words found in Luke but not found or rare in
Acts, Paul or Hebrews or *vice versa*. He recognises that in some
cases the difference may be due to difference of subject-matter
(ἐπαγγελία, καταγγέλλειν, μάρτυς common in Acts etc., rare in
Luke), but he appears not to recognise that the difference of
subject-matter extends beyond these words to whole classes of

expressions. His first set consists of πόθεν, πότε, μακρόθεν and
ὑπάγω. The first three appear four times each in Luke, not in Acts.
But the simple fact as regards the first two is that the Gospel largely
consists of short conversations abounding in direct questions, while
the Acts tends to set speeches. The nearest approach to a direct
question which could begin with 'Whence' is Acts xxiii. 34, where
however the reference to the province is necessary. μακρόθεν
occurs four time in Luke as against μάκραν three times in Acts, but
of these xxii. 54 is taken from Mark and xxiii. 49 is a reminiscence of
Ps. xxxviii. 12 in the LXX. In the other two cases μακρόθεν is definitely more appropriate than (εἰς) μάκραν would be (Luke xvi. 23
and xviii. 13). ὑπάγω he regards as peculiarly interesting, since
it is characteristic of the koine. But Luke has reduced Matthew's
twenty to six. Two are from his sources; the others come in passages
peculiar to himself, but may have been taken over from his sources,
just as in the case of ἀμήν.

Of other words rare in Acts and Paul ἀκολουθεῖν comes twenty-
five times in Matthew and is reduced to seventeen by Luke.
It occurs twice in each half of Acts. In the Gospel it occurs
twice in Lucan revisions of his sources and three times in matter
peculiar to himself; elsewhere it is taken over from the sources.
There seems no reason why Luke should have objected to the
word and his change of it is probably due to mere chance; the
comparative rarity of it in Acts is simply due to the absence of the
motif of 'following' Jesus by joining Him as a disciple in His
journeyings. Similarly ἀφιέναι (Acts three, Luke thirty-four)
largely owes its predominance to the greater frequency with which
forgiveness is referred to in the Gospel (fifteen times as against once
in Acts, but the noun ἄφεσις five times in each). In the sense of
'allow' it appears four times, all from Luke's sources; the Matthean
parallel to xii. 39 has εἴασεν, which may be assumed to be Matthew's
alteration. Luke uses ἐάω twice, in iv. 41 using it to replace Mark's
ἀφῆκεν. Probably he would have used ἐάω more often in this sense
if left to himself, since it appears seven times in Acts all in the second
half. He uses ἀφιέναι in the sense of 'leaving' twelve times, at
xv. 4 replacing it by καταλείπει (cf. Matt. xviii. 12). He might

have used the latter more often if left to himself (Acts five times, four in the second half). But there was no obvious objection to the word, and the main reason for the difference is difference of subject-matter.

βάλλω appears nineteen times as against five times in Acts (all in the second half); three times it is used of being cast into prison, in which sense it also appears three times in Acts; three times it appears in purely Lucan passages, the rest from his sources. Left to himself again he might have used ῥίπτω more often (he uses it in xvii. 2 to replace Mark's βέβληται); the word appears three times in the second half of Acts. But Acts did not want to use words meaning 'cast' as often as the Gospel.

μνημεῖον occurs ten times in Luke as against once in Acts, while μνῆμα appears three times in Luke and twice in Acts. But Acts had little need to write of tombs, whereas the tomb of Jesus figured largely in the Gospel tradition.

παιδίον appears thirteen times in Luke (so Moulton and Geden as against Clark's fourteen). Of these one (xi. 7), though peculiar to Luke, is probably from Q material omitted by Matthew. Four are from Mark and Q. The remaining seven are all from Luke's Infancy narrative. It is of interest that Luke eliminates the word from the story of Jairus's daughter, where Mark uses it four times. It is possible that Luke, if left to himself, would have used παῖς or τέκνον but the simple fact is that Acts had relatively little occasion to talk of children (παῖς once, τέκνον twice in the literal sense).

ὧδε (Luke sixteen times, Acts twice) is somewhat more in Clark's favour, since while nine times it comes from Luke's sources, in six it comes in matter peculiar to Luke; once (ix. 41) it comes in a Lucan revision of Mark in which Matthew and Luke agree; it is possible that they both had access to a variant of the story, while ὧδε in Luke is not above suspicion (cf. Streeter, *The Four Gospels*, p. 317). On the other hand in Acts ἐνθάδε appears five times as against once in Luke. But ὧδε is the normal LXX word (ἐνθάδε only twice in Greek books), and there was no reason why Luke should not retain it if it came to him in the tradition or even prefer it in his Gospel as more suitable to 'sacred prose'.

Clark next gives a group of eight words not found in the Gospels, which are found in Acts and Paul. Of these ἐλπίς, ἐπικαλεῖσθαι and παρρησιάϳεσθαι are irrelevant, since there are no occasions when the Gospel uses any synonym; the words were not needed. Luke twice uses ὑποδέχομαι where Acts has ξενίϳειν; but Acts also uses ὑποδέχομαι once (Clark ascribes it to Paul four times, but Moulton and Geden give no references to Paul!). ἡμέτερος might be interesting were it not for the fact that the figures for Acts are only three times as against none. But ἡμέτερος has strong support in Luke xvi. 12 in B, L and Origen and is distinctly the *difficilior lectio*, while in Acts xxiv. 6 it is highly doubtful. Such a difference is too small to count. κατανταν reflects the difference in the whole setting of the Gospel and the Acts. The journeys and place-settings of the Gospel are all irrelevant to the narrative, except for the triumphal entry in Mark xi. 1 and parallels, where ἐγγίϳειν was necessary. Acts represents a genuine historical tradition of events which really happened in the cities which Paul visited. All the nine cases of κατανταν occur in the second half of Acts. χρῆσθαι (twice) and μάλιστα (three times) are not significant.

The list of words rare in the Gospels but found in Acts and Paul is equally unimpressive. ἀναλαμβάνειν (eight times in Acts, not in Luke) occurs three times in the story of the Ascension, whereas the very dubious reading of Luke xxiv. 51 has ἀνεφέρετο. In Acts x. 16 it is used of the vessel let down in Peter's vision. It is used three times of Paul, being 'picked up' in his journeys and in vii. 43 in a quotation from the LXX. The Gospel had no cause to use the word. ἄχρι (Luke four times, Acts sixteen) means little. In three out of the four times it is in matter found in Luke only. Of other words, for 'until' or 'as far as', ἕως appears thirteen times in Luke, seventeen times in Acts, and μέχρι once in Luke and twice in Acts. Such terms are rarer in the Gospel than in the Acts, and in any case ἕως is the normal LXX word. βούλεσθαι (Luke twice, Acts fourteen) might be significant, but again proves far too much, since it occurs three times only in the first half of Acts as against eleven times in the second, while in v. 33 ℵ and the Western MSS. read ἐβουλεύοντο. Clark regards this word as peculiarly significant, since it was tending in the koine to give place to θέλω. The latter word appears twenty-eight times in Luke, sixteen times in Acts. Curiously enough only four of these are in the first half of Acts, for the simple reason that there was little need of either word. Eleven of the cases in which it appears in Luke are from his sources; the other cases presumably came to Luke from sources which have not survived elsewhere, and there was no reason why he should revise them since θέλω is a perfectly good word.

The comparative rarity of διό in Luke (twice, as against Acts ten) is mainly due to the difference of style between the collections of sayings of Jesus which scarcely for the most part pretend to be consecutive discourses, and the set speeches of Acts in which the particle is in place; in the rare occasions where it might be used Luke follows the διὰ τοῦτο of his sources. But at vii. 7 he introduces it in rewriting the story of the centurion's servant. διότι (Luke three times, Acts five) is insignificant. ἐπιμένειν (Luke none, Acts eight) is not a word for which there was much scope in the Gospel. The uncompounded form of the verb occurs seven times in Luke and thirteen times in Acts, and διαμένειν, which is good literary koine (Xenophon, etc.), twice. συνέρχεσθαι (Luke twice, Acts seventeen) looks striking, especially as nine out of the seventeen appearances are in the first half of Acts; but of these nine no less than five occur in the incident of Cornelius (cf. above, p. 31 f. and below, p. 106 f.). Luke uses σύνειμι in viii. 4 and συμπορεύομαι three times, but it is hard to ascribe these variations to anything but chance, the latter word being good classical Greek.

There is indeed one word in this list where the difference between Luke and Acts is significant. The word τέρας 'portent' appears nine times in Acts and not in Luke. But the change is significant not of a difference of authorship, but of a difference of atmosphere. The miracles of Jesus are never described as 'signs' or 'portents'; Jesus was asked for a sign and we know His answer. We read of 'signs' and 'portents' in Matthew and Mark, but they are to be given by false Christs.[1]

---

[1] Cf. above p. 89.

διά with the genitive (Luke fourteen, Acts fifty-one) again looks striking, and again proves on examination to be without significance. It is used of place, time, means and agents twelve times in Luke, twenty-four times in Acts. The other two cases in Luke refer to things foretold 'through' the prophets. The number rises to seven in Acts, which merely means that Luke rightly puts his testimonia here and not, as Matthew does, in the Gospel (he has thirteen instances). The rest of the surplus in Acts is due to the frequency of references to things done through Christ (or His grace or His name) through the Holy Ghost, through angels or through the hands of the Apostles. All these are phrases which do not enter the Gospel tradition.

Clark comments on the frequency of ἐάν, ὃς ἄν and ὅταν in Luke and their relative rarity in Acts (ἐάν: Luke thirty, Acts six; ὃς ἄν: Luke twenty, Acts four; ὅταν: Luke twenty-nine, Acts two). But the difference is due to the contrast between the sweeping generalisations of the preaching of Jesus and the mainly apologetic preaching of Acts, which had no need for such words. The preference of ἵνα (Luke thirty-eight, Acts twelve) to ὅπως (Luke seven, Acts fifteen) shows a remarkable curiosity. Clark notes that the preference for the latter word is shared by Matthew; but it is also shared by the first half of Acts. Of the fifteen occasions when the word occurs, seven come from the first half of Acts, eight from the second. On the other hand of the thirteen appearances of ἵνα in Acts only three come from the first half. Thus it is not surprising that ἵνα should predominate in Luke, though it must be noted that nineteen cases are drawn from his sources. Clearly no inference can be drawn unless we choose to make a somewhat bold conjecture that for some reason ὅπως was popular in the Greek-speaking Jews of Palestine.

On the use of the optative after the classical style (as noted by Blass, *Gr.N.T.Gr.* p. 220) no argument can be based; it survives in Luke in his fragments of 'scholarship prose', as does the optative in questions and conditional sentences; but these fragments are more frequent in Acts, especially in the later chapters where Luke had no sources to follow. That there are no such usages in the few fragments in the Gospel proves nothing. Similarly the ellipse of ἔφη and εἶπεν and the use of καὶ νῦν are possible in the style of conversation in Acts, but not in the style dictated to Luke by the whole Gospel tradition. Again the variation in the use of negatives has no significance. The greater frequency of μή in the Gospel (Luke ninety-four, Acts fifty-two) is largely determined by the frequency of commands in a negative form in the Gospel, whether direct or indirect in form. This difference of subject-matter accounts for fifty-one cases in the Gospel as against twenty-six in the Acts. Similarly the relative frequency of οὐ μή in the Gospel is due to the frequency of absolute prohibitions and predictions in the prophetic style proper to the Gospel but not in place in Acts. μηδείς appears nine times in the Gospel, twenty-three times in Acts, but of these only eight are in the first half, three being in the vision of Cornelius; it was a word which Luke used freely, but again did not trouble to introduce in revision of sources, even if there was an opening for it. οὐχί (Luke fifteen times, Acts twice) is a difference which is simply due to the predominance of direct speech of a conversational style in the Gospel as against Acts; it is noticeable that its prominence in Paul (seventeen times; Clark is wrong in giving twenty-two) is due to its appearing twelve times in 1 Cor., where Paul is at his most argumentative.

In regard to the choice of synonyms Clark emphasises the difference between Luke's use of ἀγρός (Luke ten, Acts once) and the use by Acts of χωρίον (Acts six, Luke none). He remarks that 'Moulton and Milligan conjecture that ἀγρός was a favourite word with scribes who were translating from a semitic original, but this does not seem convincing'. A glance at Hatch and Redpath's *Concordance of the LXX* shows that the scribes who translated the LXX use χωρίον twice, the Greek books four times; references to ἀγρός occupy three columns with about seventy-five references to the column. It is difficult to see why Moulton and Milligan's statement should be advanced with such diffidence, or what measure of numerical preponderance would be needed to carry conviction. In any case all but two of Luke's uses come from his sources (the remaining two from the Prodigal Son). We have a clear case of Luke's use of 'sacred prose'.

In regard to words for 'killing' (ἀναιρεῖν; Luke twice, Acts

nineteen; ἀποκτείνειν: Luke thirteen, Acts twice), Luke twice
substitutes ἀναιρεῖν for Mark's ἀποκτείνειν; of his uses of ἀποκτείνειν,
seven come from his sources, and two (xi. 47 f.) from a passage in
which Luke seems to be nearer the original of the Q passage than
Matthew. Somewhat curiously Clark includes the word ἀπολλύναι
(Luke twenty-eight, Acts twice). But the word means to lose or to
destroy (whether by killing or otherwise) or in its passive forms to
perish. Of Luke's uses thirteen mean 'lose' (souls, sheep, coins,
prodigal sons, etc.), seven to perish, five to destroy (of demons,
which cannot be killed and properly cannot be destroyed, though
they can be neutralised by imprisonment in the abyss; of souls, and
of destruction by floods or fires from heaven), three could mean to
kill in the sense that they refer to destruction by killing, but of these
two (xi. 51 and xiii. 33) are in the passive form and mean rather to
perish. In xix. 47 the scribes seek to destroy Jesus by killing Him;
but the sentence is taken from Mark. Of the two uses in Acts one
refers to Judas of Galilee, who 'perished' by being killed; the other
refers to 'a hair of your head'.

Of words for 'speaking', λαλεῖν (Luke thirty, Acts sixty-three)
owes its predominance in Acts to the subject-matter, since it is
regularly used of God or the Holy Spirit speaking through prophets,
of speaking with tongues, of speaking 'the word' or 'in the name of
Jesus'. φάναι (Acts twenty-seven, Luke six) occurs six times only
in the first half of Acts and three of these are in the incident of
Cornelius. Matthew has a curious fondness for the word, using it
seventeen times; Luke does not trouble to revise his sources in this
respect. The preponderance of εἰπεῖν and λέγειν in the Gospel as
against Acts is of course determined by the subject-matter. In
regard to verbs for knowing the only serious difference noted by
Clark is the frequency of ἐπίστασθαι (Acts ten, Luke none); but
these are all in the second half, except for x. 28 (the incident of
Cornelius).

The common words noted by Clark as peculiar to the Gospel are
for the most part too rarely used in Luke to have any significance.
It is curious that ὁμοίως should not occur in Acts, but on the one or
two occasions when the subject-matter would have permitted it, the

writer employs some other turn of phrase as in i. 11. μείζων (seven times in Luke) owes its relative frequency to the disputes for precedence among the disciples (four times). His list of words 'which indicate the expression of emotion' found in the Gospel and absent from Acts shows nothing except that the purpose of the Gospel is to record the teaching of Jesus and to give a picture of Him, while the purpose of Acts is to describe the spread of Christianity in a manner which will make the book an effective apologia. There was little opening for ἐπιτιμᾶν in Acts, since in the Gospel it is largely employed of the miraculous rebuking of winds and demons, or of Jesus's rebukes addressed to His disciples; it might have been employed in such a passage as Acts viii. 20 or xiii. 9, but it implies a measure of superiority of the giver of the rebuke to the recipient which is rare in Acts.

Similarly Clark's comment for the rarity of words for eating, drinking, etc. disappears when it is observed that of the words he quotes, ἀμπελών, δεῖπνον and καρπός are confined to parables and parabolic expressions; these account for four out of six uses of οἶνος, ten out of seventeen uses of πίνειν and four out of five of πεινᾶν. This word might have been used at Acts x. 10, but for some reason Luke preferred the curious periphrasis. Clark's figures for ἐσθίειν seem to have been drawn from a concordance which gave the past tense φαγεῖν under a separate heading; the correct figures would seem to be thirty-three for the Gospel and six for the Acts. But here we must allow for the large part played in the Gospel over rabbinical debates as to eating with publicans and the argument over eating corn picked on the sabbath (six cases); it happens that the only debate on the subject in Acts uses συνεσθίειν; by parables and parabolic expressions (eleven cases); the Last Supper (five cases); the resulting difference is simply due to the subject-matter. Clark's last selection of words indicating rank, beauty or wealth shows: δοῦλος, Gospel twenty-seven, Acts three, where twenty out of Luke's twenty-seven are in parables or similar expressions; καλός (Gospel nine, Acts none), where seven of the cases come from parables or similar expressions, and the word only means 'beautiful' as against 'good' in xxi. 5; πλούσιος (Gospel eleven, Acts none), where six are from parables, while Acts does not breathe the economic quarrels of rich and poor on the soil of Palestine; and πτωχός (Gospel ten, Acts none), where four cases are from parables, while the rest emanate from the situation of the Gospels, in which Jesus preaches the Gospel primarily to the poor. Clark's inference that the author of Acts took little interest in rank, beauty or wealth is curious in view of the writer's care to mention the conversion of those of good social status in xiii. 12, xvii. 4, 12 and 34, and xix. 31. It might indeed be urged that this is inconsistent with the emphasis of the Gospel on the value of poverty; but the most ardent Christian Socialist is liable to feel a certain thrill when he finds a duchess in his congregation.

INDEX

I. CLASSICAL WRITERS

II. THE OLD TESTAMENT

III. JEWISH WRITERS

IV. THE NEW TESTAMENT

V. CHRISTIAN WRITERS

VI. MODERN WRITERS

VII. NAMES AND SUBJECTS

grand theme of Prophets: Idolatry, the worshipping of dead Idols as the Divinity, is a thing they cannot away-with, but have to denounce continually, and brand with inexpiable reprobation; it is the chief of all the sins they see done under the sun. This is worth noting. We will not enter here into the theological question about Idolatry. Idol is *Eidolon*, a thing seen, a symbol. It is not God, but a Symbol of God; and perhaps one may qestion whether any the most benighted mortal ever took it for more than a Symbol. I fancy, he did not think that the poor image his own hands had made *was* God; but that God was emblemed by it, that God was in it some way or another. And now in this sense, one may ask, Is not all worship whatsoever a worship by Symbols, by *eidola*, or things seen? Whether *seen*, rendered visible as an image or picture to the bodily eye; or visible only to the inward eye, to the imagination, to the intellect: this makes a superficial, but no substantial difference. It is still a Thing Seen, significant of Godhead; an Idol. The most rigorous Puritan has his Confession of Faith, and intellectual Representation of Divine things, and worships thereby; thereby is worship first made possible for him. All creeds, liturgies, religious forms, conceptions that fitly invest religious feelings, are in this sense *eidola*, things seen. All worship whatsoever must proceed by Symbols, by Idols:—we may say, all Idolatry is comparative, and the worst Idolatry is only *more* idolatrous.

Where, then, lies the evil of it? some fatal evil must lie in it, or earnest prophetic men would not on all hands so reprobate it. Why is Idolatry so hateful to Prophets? It seems to me as if, in the worship of those poor wooden symbols, the thing that had chiefly provoked the Prophet, and filled his inmost soul with indignation and aversion, was not exactly what suggested itself to his own thought, and came out of him in words to others, as the thing. The rudest heathen that worshipped Canopus, or the Caabah Black-Stone, he, as we saw, was superior to the horse that worshipped nothing at all! Nay there was a kind of lasting merit in that poor act of his; analogous to what is still meritorious in Poets: recognition of a certain endless